LAST MINUTE EMAILS TO **GOD** FROM A DYING UNBELIEVER

Dear God, Which Way Is Up?

From the Dear God Can We Chat Series

ELIZABETH BELL

Trilogy Christian Publishers
A Wholly Owned Subsidary of Trinity Broadcasting Network
2442 Michelle Drive
Tustin, CA 92780

Copyright © 2020 by Elizabeth Bell

All rights reserved, including the right to reproduce this book or portions thereof in any form whatsoever.

For information, address Trilogy Christian Publishing
Rights Department, 2442 Michelle Drive, Tustin, Ca 92780.
Trilogy Christian Publishing/ TBN and colophon are trademarks of Trinity Broadcasting Network.

For information about special discounts for bulk purchases, please contact Trilogy Christian Publishing.

Manufactured in the United States of America

Trilogy Disclaimer: The views and content expressed in this book are those of the author and may not necessarily reflect the views and doctrine of Trilogy Christian Publishing or the Trinity Broadcasting Network.

10 9 8 7 6 5 4 3 2 1

Library of Congress Cataloging-in-Publication Data is available.

ISBN 978-1-64088-239-3 (Print Book)
ISBN 978-1-64088-240-9 (ebook)

Unless otherwise indicated, all scripture quotations are taken from the *King James Version* of the Bible. Concepts with supporting scriptures have been asterisked (*) to indicate that they appear either in in the footnotes, or the Endnotes section in the back of this book. A review of the account of the fall of Adam, as recorded in the book of Genesis, will support reader comprehension.

Scripture quotations marked (NIV) are taken from the Holy Bible, New International Version®, NIV®. Copyright © 1973, 1978, 1984, 2011 by Biblica, Inc.™ Used by permission of Zondervan. All rights reserved worldwide. www. zondervan.com The "NIV" and "New International Version" are trademarks registered in the United States Patent and Trademark Office by Biblica, Inc.™

Scripture verses marked (NKJV) are from the New King James Version®. Copyright © 1982 by Thomas Nelson. Used by permission. All rights reserved.

Scripture quotations taken from the New American Standard Bible® (NASB), Copyright © 1960, 1962, 1963, 1968, 1971, 1972, 1973,1975, 1977, 1995 by The Lockman Foundation. Used by permission. www.Lockman.org

Scripture quotations marked (CEV) are from the Contemporary English Version Copyright © 1991, 1992, 1995 by American Bible Society. Used by Permission.

The Holy Bible, Berean Study Bible, BSB
Copyright ©2016, 2018 by Bible Hub
Used by Permission. All Rights Reserved Worldwide.

My style with the "Feisty" Unbeliever? Lots of patience. Lots of laughter. A bit of tough love...with a few tears.

Hoping to become the Proud "New Birth" Father!
—God

I used to blame God for not fixing humanity's problems. But now I understand the power of Adamic choice. For heaven to get Personally involved is such an amazing gift!
Amazed by Grace—for Me

Heaven just became much more real and wonderful.
—Top Floor, Please
—Going Up!

I've never had the courage to confess my confusion about the "God stuff," about Jesus. As a "closet-doubter" Christian, I've even questioned my need for the Cross. But, Dear God, Which Way Is Up? *gave me fresh vision about the deity of Christ. And like the doubting disciple who touched His nailed-scarred hands, I believe!*
—Fully Persuaded

Wonderfully complex! Yet easy to understand! What is God's email address?
—Generation Z, Twenty Something

Last Minute—completely changed my "No God" point of view. I want to go up! Atheist, no more!

A masterpiece for troubled times! *This book is AMAZING!*

—*Grace*

Substantially delightful!!! Father and I Are pleased with how I was handled in this book. Thank you, Holy Spirit for helping the author present...

—*The Word*

Special Acknowledgments

Matt and Laurie ~ As the urgency for the gospel to be spread throughout the world increases, thank you for your continued faithfulness. The World-Wide Evangelism tool your parents, Paul and Jan Crouch, started is a great contribution to humanity—and is needed, especially at this time." In Christ, Elizabeth Bell, the Author.

Dr. Mitchell:

Your guidance supported my acceptance into the Doctoral Program in Organizational Leadership at the University of San Francisco. It also contributed to my ability to complete *Dear God, Which Way is Up?* While in your program, I learned that if I kept writing long enough, I would eventually finish my course. So, I kept writing, and my book was picked up by TBN! Thank you.

In honor of your 50 years in education: 42 years of exemplary service at USF, and 8 years prior as a classroom teacher in Maryland, I join those throughout our nation who applaud you.

You kept writing on hearts and lives to impact educational and life change—and now, you too, have finished *your course!* Such a distinguished accomplishment!

Dr. Patricia Mitchell, Well done!

48 Hours 'til Eternity

(Throughout this text, God's Words are presented in italics **and the Dying Unbeliever's in regular font).**

Excuse me, please! Am I headed in the right
direction? I'm trying to get to heaven?
Which road are you taking?
My OWN path!
*NO! Pull off at the next exit! If you keep
heading your way, you'll end up lost!*
ETERNALLY?

Yep!

GOD

From first Adam the fallen—to Second Adam
the Risen—and then of course, there's you! This
exciting journey is one you don't want to miss! Bring
your "God" questions—on your mark, Get set.
Ready! Go! Come only if you want to be sure!

from *the Dear God, Can We Chat Series*

by E. E. Blessings

To: God

From: A Dying Unbeliever

Dear God,

With less than 48 hours to live—now, alone—I weigh more carefully my rejection of Your Son's claim that He's the only way that leads to You.

To the exclusion of all other options, His statement, "I am the way, the truth and the life and no one comes to the Father, but by Me," remains far too narrow for my embrace. So, I've chosen an alternative path!

My arrangements to come to You upon my death have been finalized. However, I plan to come through a different god, and on other terms. I believe there are multiple roads that lead to Heaven where multiple gods will reign!

But I recently heard there's only One Risen Savior Who'll reign as Lord in Your Kingdom. Who is He? And why would there be such exclusivity regarding Who will reign as "King of Kings?"

Is it only **Your** Son Who qualifies to fulfill this Royally exclusive role?

If so, would the exclusivity of His claim align with the exclusivity of His rule and reign with You—triumphantly—and throughout all eternity?

And can He alone cleanse those who will be granted inclusion in Your Kingdom—having done Your Perfect Will, as Your Eternal Word?

I must admit, I thought Your Son was only a suffering servant. I never knew He is a Reigning King with Majesty and Kingdom authority, and that He holds all Power in Heaven and on Earth in His nail-scarred Hands!

Currently considering if I should adjust my perspective to be more discerning of His. And that I should hail, rather than reject such a Worthy Sovereign, especially if it is to *Him* that I must bow.

I do want excellent eternal accommodations when I die! So…

I

Dear God, Can We Chat?

Dear Dying Unbeliever,

I'd love to!

God

Oh Good!

Then I'll just jump right in! To be perfectly honest, I do have a growing number of concerns.

I've enjoyed a good life on this side and would like a comfortable one where I'll be headed in just a few hours. So, I'd like to know if there's still time for me to reconsider Your Son? You see, it's bothering me that when I completely dismissed Him, I had no idea He's quite as significant, as it appears, He might be! So...

Dear God,

Your Son hasn't dismissed me also, has He?

Dear Dying Unbeliever,

Indeed not! And yes! There is still time!

Oh, Great!

Just wanted to make sure the gates to Your House are still open to me and I can still move in!

I've run late for important appointments just about my whole life, and it looks like I'm running late now.

As You can imagine, moving to heaven is a really big deal for most folks down here! And to be totally transparent, with each passing hour, I'm feeling quite less and less prepared! In fact, I'm getting a little worried about the cost.

So…

Dear God,

Is there a payment required to move into Your House?

Dear Dying Unbeliever,

Yes! There is!

Oh no! Dear God,

I am so broke! And really embarrassed because I've blown *so* much of my money when I should've saved! Had I saved even a little, I would be in a much better position to come up with at least a small down payment toward my move-in fees.

Dear Anxious One,

You did not let Me finish.

There is a payment required, but My Son already paid your move-in debt in full!

In full? Re-e-eally God? Your Son paid it all?

Yes! Dying Unbeliever!

It was a bloody, painful price but, He paid It all!

Dear God!

Please tell Him thank you! And what a relief!

Your Son sounds so kind and caring, and quite sacrificial. And I would imagine He's a *very* special Man.

But, to be fair to my god of choice—if this debt has to be paid by a deity—I think records might show that my god has already covered—at least partially—my move-in fees. No disrespect to Your Son's contribution, but as a loyal follower,

I'd better accept what my god might've already paid toward my eternal accommodations!

Eternal accommodations? *In My House?*

Dear Dying Unbeliever,

The only God qualified to pay the debt you must settle before moving into My House—is My Son!

Oh! My!

You're really picky, aren't You, God? So, what kind of a debt is it?

"In-debted" Unbeliever,

It's a debt owed by ALL humanity.

You mean EVERY person owes this Debt?

And must pay! But My Son's Debt-Forgiveness and Cleansing Services—although available to all—cover only those who will receive Him! For there are so many who reject My Son!

So-o-o...

Would that mean His "Whosoever Will" Package provides **inclusion,** but with a hint of **exclusion**—for all who *refuse* His provision?

That's right!—to be fairly balanced with a side of consequence or reward! For all who receive Him will be received by Him.

But those who reject Him, God?

Well, Dying Unbeliever,

*It's simple math! Since My Son is the only One who paid the debt for humanity to establish permanent residency in My House, only **He** sets humanity's move-in terms!*

Only **He** sets the terms? But what about His **BAD** math?

Dear God!

Your Son subtracts all the paths that lead to You down to only One—**Himself!** So, for an equation of fair compromise, do You think He'd allow for just **some** exceptions?

I mean for the sake of those like me who don't quite agree with **His math,** or His terms?

Exceptions to allow those who disagree with Him to move into His Father's House—and bypass Him?

Dying Unbeliever,

He's My Eternal Son!!!

But He makes such **unreasonable** demands! And He really tends to be…

…Biased?

Oh, quite biased! Like He's the *only* God with the authority to allow people to come to You!

But…p-l-e-a-se don't think I want to eliminate Him completely! I mean, **Eternal Son** speaks for itself! And, I know He's a *great* option for those who can handle His style! But, as for me? Well—I'd think He'd be just a little more willing to allow…

Room for those who want to come to Me—but through a different door?

Of **per-son-al** choice!

Dear God! I couldn't've said it better myself! The "no one comes to the Father, but by me" part is just *way* too narrow a point of view!

A **broader** path…

Dying Unbeliever,

*A **broader** path—is not recommended!*

No—? (pondering) Well, maybe not—but it probably would make for a ***much*** more enjoyable trip!!

But wait! I'm not asking You to side with me—*completely*—about Your Son. But You don't agree with His, "I am the way, the truth and the life…" claim, do You?

Dying Unbeliever,

I do—fully!

Fully? With **NO** room for compromise? **W-h-o** does that?

I do that! You see, in My House, heaven does not operate by earth's standards! So, when it comes to My Son—I do not negotiate!

So sorry, God!

I didn't mean to offend You—but non-negotiables*?*

—are required in matters of life and death! And for that reason, My Son and all His terms remain <u>non</u>-negotiable.

Well. I can see **that!** I mean in matters of life and death! But, how does that apply to Your Son's payment of <u>my</u> debt?

Dying Unbeliever—My Son died!

Oh! My God! **Excuse me?** I am s-o-o sorry for Your loss! But, wait a minute! You're not talking money, You're talking death! What I owed, but He paid—required His death?

*Yes! With the **only** other option being the Eternal Death of ALL humanity!*

Well, dear God!

If Your Son gave His life for **that** cause, I can kinda see His point for standing His ground, and not wanting to take *ANY* of this lightly!

But, wait a minute—if He's dead wouldn't He basically be out of the game?

I know I'm not the sharpest knife in the drawer, and no disrespect intended but, *dead is dead!*

So, clarification please! Which is He now—dead, or alive?

*Dying Unbeliever. My Son is **ALIVE!***

ALIVE? Well shut the **"died-alive"** door!

Ex-cuse Me?

Oh no, dear God!

Please excuse me. I didn't intend to be disrespectful, but how do You explain *that* one?

He was dead?

But now He's alive??? Your Son pulled off His Own *Personal* Resurrection?

Dying Unbeliever,

My Son IS the Resurrection!!!

He is? I mean, is He?

Well...Dear God,

If Your Son is <u>ALL</u> that, then can He resurrect me?

Case in point! You being His Father and all, I would imagine getting up out of the grave *could* be possible for Him! But does His Resurrection Power also apply to me?

Because, as You know...

Confidentially, God *(Typing quietly)* I'm the one who's dying!

Very Confidentially, Dying Unbeliever,

That's why you need to understand why My Son, and only My Son, can rescue you out of the experience of eternal death, where you will find yourself if you don't make a willful course-correction.

And soon!

You see, Specially Loved Unbeliever, it's time that I share with you the backstory, to help you understand how you, and all of humanity ended up in a deadly situation!

But, dear God,

That sounds so *serious!*

Dying Unbeliever,

That's because it is!

Thank You, God for being willing to take this time out with me.

I know sometimes I tend to get off-track, and can be very self-willed.

Which leads me right into Adam.

II

Dear God,

You mean Adam was self-willed—like Me?

Dying Unbeliever,

No. You are self-willed—like Adam.

And it was the self-will—in conflict with My will—that created humanity's debt!

Such a debt that none among fallen humanity was able to make the payment that was due![1]

Dear God,

Are you s-u-r-e **I was** in on this? I might be broke, but I do pay my bills, and I don't recall contributing anything to humanity's debt—ever!

Dying Unbeliever,

*I Am certain **you are** in on this!*

No disrespect, God,

But I do believe a verification check with Your Unpaid Debts Department will show that my account *is* both current and clear*!*

Mistaken Unbeliever,

*Your account is neither current **nor** clear! Second Adam*—the only One who I've assigned to work in the Eternal Debt Removals Department—indicates no cleansing has ever been applied to your account.*

*Second Adam is another name for God's Son, Jesus Christ. (I Corinthians 15:45; 15:22).

In fact, a recent review of records shows His substitutionary payment, made on your behalf, was offered, but refused! Thus, your account is in delinquent status and will be turned over to Eternal Debt Collections for non-payment, at the time of your final breath.

Good Lord! I wonder if I've been a victim of identity theft?

No. Dying Unbeliever.

*But fallen Adam—the universal father of fallen humanity—through a willful act of disobedience—completely shattered **his** uncorrupt identity in Me.*

Consequently, as one of Adam's universal offspring, at your birth, instead of receiving **My** *identity, you inherited* **h-i-s** *broken identity—as your original father.*

Original father?

Dear God!

Broken Adam is my original dad?

I've **always** wanted to do a genealogical search to determine from whom I'm a descendant.

Are you **absolutely** sure *fallen* Adam is my original papa?

Dying Unbeliever,

You look just like him!

Then I'll just call original dad, "papa" for short!

Dear God!

Papa fell, and I look just like him?

Well, gee thanks! I guess?

But wait a minute. That's not a compliment, is it? What kind of a fall was it?

Dying Unbeliever!

It was a major catastrophe!

A major catastrophe?

Dear God!!!

What happened?

Dear Dying Unbeliever—it's quite a complicated story!

Complicated?

[Yawning] Kinda juicy??? P-l-e-ase tell me, God.

[Stretching] Tell me about my papa. Pre-tty please?

Dear Stretching and Yawning Unbeliever,

Okay, but <u>only</u> if you can stay awake.

I promise, God! There's a full charge on my laptop. It's plugged in, and I just sat up to make sure I won't start nodding.

Good! Well—here's what happened.

[Immediate yawning starts up, again.]

Sleepy Unbeliever!

Yes, Sir?

LAST MINUTE EMAILS TO GOD FROM A DYING UNBELIEVER

Think you can stay awake?

[Embarrassed] Yes, Sir.

Then here we go.

Note: Scriptures that support biblically based claims appear at the end of some chapters, and in the Endnotes section in the back of this book. The (*) identifies where scriptural support is included.

III

Through a willful act of rebellion, first-man Adam fell into a pre-existing rebellion with Satan who—had already fallen!

*In Heaven, My Home, the place where I hold complete dominion—Lucifer became outraged because—as God—I will **not** share the Exclusivity of My Authority with another god—. Certainly, not in My own Home!*

*So, he attempted to orchestrate **My Fall**. Lucifer and a third of the angels—**EACH** of them—My created, but now corrupted beings—joined forces to take **Me** down.*

"You will be like God" is the lie he told interested angels to strengthen his rebellion. It is also **the word of deception** he would later promise to lure Eve. His crafty attacks against **My Eternal Will,** through his opposition to **My Eternal Word in Heaven**—caused the corrupted angels to be ensnared into eternal death. Through masterful deception, that trickster later secured Eve's influence to ensnare distracted Adam*—the one who I gave My Word of Instruction to obey—before forming Eve from his rib.**

In the Court of Eternal Justice where I My Rule, My Sovereign Determination was decided. A fair consequence for Lucifer's defiance was to be driven out of My House! So for his hostile deed, he was sentenced to live eternally cut-off from the presence of My light, life and everlasting peace, since now My archenemy!

*And now, as **a fallen god,** FULLY equipped with power over transgression and death, Satan started his reign of rebellion with fallen dominion authority, in **his** new home—the dark domain.*

For it was through his prideful self-exaltation, and the worshipping of himself as god, that Lucifer became the fallen false god who would oppose My Throne, not only in Heaven, but also on earth, and under the earth.

I did not contest the fall of the angels, since those rebellions were fully aware of their entry into Lucifer's defiant opposition against Me—and had operated with devious intent.

But when Satan cunningly crafted a similar situation that influenced My close friend to also join in with his hostility against Me! Causing Adam to oppose My Word—the Eternal Part of Me that expresses My Will. I sent My Word to defeat Satan's crafty maneuver!

I knew Adam had rebelled!

I knew Adam had willfully gone astray!

I knew he had joined Eve—the first partaker of the forbidden experience.

And I knew she had received Satan's deceiving words, as truth, with unsuspecting acceptance, having been tricked!

But I also knew humanity's first parents did not desire entry into the deceiver's hostile defiance. Nor did they desire eternal separation away from Me, through Satan's rebellion and death.

*I knew they did **not** act with devious intent. **Nor did Adam intend to lead humanity into death.***

So, as Father God, I arranged for ALL those "willing," among humanity's fallen—to be returned back to life in Me through the victory purchased during a Bloody Battle fought at the Cross.

For—Adam's captivity into eternal death—like Satan's—was not false imprisonment—but fair and binding. Therefore, Adam's penalty of death had to be carried out as a requirement of My Eternal Justice.

So, it was with loving nail-scarred Hands, that My Son paid Adam's debt in FULL. Making Him humanity's ONLY way of escape back to eternal life in Me.

*And now, through the Second Adam's gift of eternal life— humanity faces TWO Eternal Options—**continued** captivity or **purchased** release?*

It is the "ONE-vote" heart's decision that I will honor, with eternal consequence, or reward.

For Two Kingdoms are at War!

The fallen god…still opposing the Sovereign King!

Both battling to be seated—

Exclusively—on the throne

*Of the kingdom of **each** heart—*

As Lord!

For STILL on earth

As it is in Heaven

I will

Have NO other gods

before Me!

*Endnotes

IV

WAR? Now, that woke me up, God! Do You mean there's a **REAL** WAR going on?

Yes! Battling Unbeliever,

This War of Kingdoms is VERY REAL, and is still being fought with fury, to THIS day.

*It's a super-natural, Spiritual War reflected in the natural world, and impacts ones life—**or** death, every day!*

Do You mean even as far as **today,** God?

But, How could such a s-i-m-p-le battle over my papa last SO long?

Dear underestimator of the Complexity of Humanity's Spiritual War!

*There's **nothing** simple about the devastation caused by Adam's fall! The war is complex, and Satan is cunning! His desire is to* *keep humanity in **his** possession, and to stop humanity's return back to life in Me.*

I don't get it God! Since You've got the Super Power advantage, why didn't You just squash Your enemy right out the gate—before he could gather his troops to fight against You?

Dying Unbeliever,

Only few understand—that I view the affairs of eternity from Heaven's perspective, and make decisions based on My Eternal Will!

Which is why, I've given haughty Satan a limited window of time to continue his fight against My Sovereign Plan before I'll lock him away—eternally.

Because its EVEN his opposing presence that works together with My Established Purpose to help fulfill My Sovereign Will,— which is to allow humanity to choose either life in Me, or willful separation!

*You see, **Willfully** Separated Unbeliever,*

Forced compliance of the will does not define my Eternal Style.

In fact, I could have created Adam and Eve as robots, forcefully pre-programmed to walk obediently with Me, as their God.

But as the loving heavenly Father, what I desire is a committed family made up of children who draw near to Me from hearts of grateful commitment…and who love Me deeply because that's how I love the world!

Those who stay away from Me—willfully—are not Mine.

So for the sake of each individual electing their "eternal family affiliation"—while on earth—through personal decision, I gave humanity free choice!

V

Y-e-s!!! Free Choice! PRO-CHOICE! God, I didn't know You're PRO-CHOICE? Totally **freeing!**

Oh, Yes! "Choosing" Unbeliever.

Absolutely, Yes! I'm Pro-ETERNAL Choice!

Pro-Eternal Consequence!

And Pro-Eternal Reward!

Now, wait, God! ALL Three?

Dying Unbeliever, Yep!

*Oh, and—here's a little more information about your original dad, and **"his**-choice." Adam was plainly duped when he chose the forbidden path. But the death he experienced came because he didn't pay close enough attention to the deadly **consequence of his choice**.*

So, let's see—papa wasn't factoring in consequences, God?

Nope. Which is why I felt Adam's pain so deeply when he found out with sorrow, tears, and regret—

that a willful "free" choice that opposes My Word will result in unexpected death!

Unexpected death??? **Dear** God!

What happened?

Dying Unbeliever,

*Soon after Adam abandoned **My** path, and entered into Satan's deadly trap, tragedy touched his family.*

H-o-w, God?

It was devastating! Adam's angry son, Cain, killed his bother, Abel!

Papa's son committed the first homicide?? Two brothers? **My** uncles? Oh, no! Poor papa.

*And when Adam cried to me in agony, "Murder in **MY** family? God!!! Where did **this** HORROR come from?" It was hard for Me to see him suffer such **deep** pain!.*

ALL this came from FREE CHOICE, God?

Dying Unbeliever, Yes.

*THIS was the outcome of Adam's **"free"** decision! His **"freeing decision,"** that allowed him to wilfully disobey My Instructions,* *painfully led to tragic death and separation from his beloved sons! Which is why when I looked into Adam's weeping eyes, I was reminded that one day—for Adam—I would have to separate from Mine!*

Oh, NO! Looks like "Not-so-free" papa got in touch with pain and trouble!

Dear "Not-So-Free" Unbeliever,

*But Adam's trouble IMMEDIATELY got in touch with **heaven!***

Really, God? So, what did Heaven **do?**

Dying Unbeliever.

Heaven came down to personally engage in Adam's war!!!

VI

(Raises hand) I got a question, God…

Why did heaven fight for papa? Was he an influential man?

Dear Child of Adam's Seed,

Adam was a VERY influential man!

I made him just a little lower than the angels, but with a superior ability—to procreate. Which is Adam's participation with Me in the start-up of new-born human life. By depositing My "life-giving" blood into a mother's womb——at first Adam, and then his immediate sons, followed by his universal sons— would initiate the start-up of new life, and children would be multiplied. As the Creator, I gave the first man the power for a powerful "creation collaboration" between us!

Wow God!

You gave papa co-creative power to work with You? Then, y-e-s, papa **was** highly **in-flu-en-tial**!

Yes, "Child Born of a Mother and One of Adam's Sons"!

And when Adam deposited his "life-giving" blood into Eve, initiating the start-up of humanity's first birth—this established "the original two" as humanity's first and universal parents. For Adam and Eve's sons, and then their sons, so forth and so on— passed on Adam's univesal bloodline that travels on to this day, through the mothers of the earth.

Dear God,

This is a **little** embarrassing, but I think what You're describing is referred to as the sperm being passed to the egg! I learned that in Biology. And I **don't** think we'll need to go into the rest, God!

Dear Embarrassed One,

Let's not.

Good enough! But before we move on, here's one more thing I learned in school related to a new birth!

Dear God,

I learned that the father's sperm carries the blood that fertilizes the mother's egg. Therefore, the father and his baby's blood-type match up, and that's why paternity tests work.

*Um hum! (Quietly ponders His Son's birth) Yep! And since His Father's "blood" initiated the start-up of **His** birth, a Paternity test would show that **My** "blood type" matched **perfectly** with His "life-giving, life-cleansing" blood that My Son carried to the earth, as Mary's Baby.*

God, are we talking about the same thing?

Nope!

I didn't think so. We'll then, I'll just finish my thought!

So a baby, although carried by the mother, can act **just** like the father, and even look **just** like the father, since the baby shares the father's genetic DNA, passed on by the father' blood.

Yes!!! Just like Me and My Only Begotten Son! I sent Him down to earth, carrying a fresh and pure allotment of Heaven's blood, unstained by Adam's sin.

Dying Unbeliever,

Do you know what that says about you?

No—God, What?

*It means you were born with **Adam's condemnation, having inherited his "tainted" blood,** as a carrier of the "universal sin virus!" Therefore, you are in need of a Blood Transfusion from the Second Adam in order to be cleansed.*

Dear God,

I'm sure that's W-A-Y **too deep** for me!

Dying Unbeliever, Yep.

*Adam's stain is a **very deep** experience!*

*Oh, **MY!***

VII

Dear Dying Unbeliever,

The Adams were VERY strategic-in-purpose "earth m/Men!"

My Son, Second Adam, was the only Man born through a virgin earthen-dust vessel, into whom I poured My rich deposit of "purifying, life-cleansing" blood.

*First Adam was the **only** man created out of the dust, into whom I poured My rich deposit of pure "life-giving" blood.*

*And it was out of **"One Blood"**—Adam's "one-blood" deposit that I made ALL nations.* And I placed life in the blood.***

*So, when Adam contaminated his life with evil, through the rebellion of sin that leads to death, Adam entered into death—and in Adam **all** die.*

A-L-L must die? But, why God?

Dying Unbeliever,

*Because humanity's "filthied by sin" condition required its eternal and TOTAL separation from Me. You see, ALL of Adam's children would be born into Adam's captivity of death—and rebellion and death **cannot live** in Me.*

Total separation, God? But, I thought said You were my papa's Close Friend! So—how could You allow a total separation from him?

Did You stop loving my papa because He got all dirtied up, God?

So Loved Unbeliever,

*I loved Adam deeply, **even** in his filthy condition.*

*But I **could NOT** allow Adam to pollute Me, as God—the Father, with His deadly decision. Therefore, after Adam's fall, we separated. **For Adam went his own way!!! The way of sin and death.***

So, God, is there ANY hope?

Yep, but only through a Pure Blood Transfusion from a Purifying Outside Source. For ONLY with "cleansed" blood, returned back to its ORIGINAL state of pure life—will I allow Adam's family to be re-connected back to new life in Me!! For I Am Pure, and I Am Life.

Good grief!

Then, fat chance for a **second chance,** God!

And shame on papa for dirtying up the family's bloodline! Now, **EVERYBODY** needs a blood transfusion! And I just know Pure-Blood that washes away smelly stains probably HAS to be expensive!!!

Yes. Dying Unbeliever,

The high cost for shedding Blood with 'life-cleansing' Power was ***astronomical!***

And MY Son died to give IT!

So, it IS out of "One "Spiritual" Blood"—Second Adam's "One-Blood" deposit—that I Am forming MY "CLEANSED NEW-LIFE" Nation! For I placed "Blood-Cleansing" additives in My Son's blood that He shed. Consequently, it can purify any "sin-stained" life.

YOU MEAN MY PAPA MADE YOUR SON GIVE BLOOD?

Then shame on papa for doin' DIRT!

*And He has made from one blood every nation of men to dwell on all the face of the earth. Acts 17:26 New King James Version

*From one man he made all the nations(.) Acts 17:26 New International Version

**For the life of the flesh is in the blood." Leviticus 17:11

VIII

Dear Dying Unbeliever,

Do you know what I wanted in Adam?

What, God?

A Forever Family.

A what?

I wanted a Forever Family that would live eternally with Me, since connected to Me through father Adam—the original man in whom I entrusted pure-connecting life!

Then, God, it's a good thing You have SUPER-DUPER GOD Powers! And despite papa's **bad** blood, You can turn ALL humanity into Your BIG HAPPY family—someday through an **a-m-a-z-i-n-g** AUTOMATIC **"Operation New-life"** Campaign!

You're able to do that, r-i-g-h-t God?

Wrong!

Dying Unbeliever,

*Because of Adam's fall, things will never be amazing outside of grace!! And birth into my "Forever Family" will **never** be a-u-t-o-m-a-t-i-c! Nor can ones decision to willingly join My Family **ever** be determined by Me.*

…but why, God? Why don't you EVER use YOUR **Super-Duper—Potent-Totent—Omni-Bomni** God Power?

*I do! (Although, I've never looked at My Power q-u-i-t-e like **THAT.**)*

*But, it's through the wooing touch of the Power of My Spirit— that I help influence "Forever Family-Life-Changing" decisions, one **willing** birth at a time!*

It's choice! Dying Unbeliever,

*Clear-cut choice!! EACH individual must **choose** to move out of Adamic condemnation and into new-life conversion—**or not.** For its only through the acceptance of My Word that human- ity can return to Me. You see, Willful Unbeliever—acceptance or rejection of the "whosoever **will**—come," Family Invitation* that's been sent out to EVERYONE is a matter of personal choice.*

A family invitation? EVERYONE?

Dear God!

Did I miss **the** invite?

Was this invitation sent via group email? WHEN was it **sent,** God? Was I copied on? Why wasn't I COPIED O-N?

Note to self: calm down!!!

But what have I missed? Why was I **excluded** from the "Forever Family Invitation? WHO S-E-N-T IT??? **Why, God why-y-y-y**—was I excluded???

Note to self: **breathe-e-e!**

DEAR GOD!

We BOTH know I have **exclusion issues!** Remember? I a-m **nev-er** a happy camper when I'm NOT in the loop—And right about now, I feel **SO** left outside in the dark!

God, would you answer—PLEASE?

(Frantically dialing) Please answer! I'm calling Your **4-1-1 Help line! Hello, Hello! IN-FOR-MA-TION, Please!**

About this Invitation to the Nation! I need—

IN-FOR-MA-TION! Please!!!

*Behold, I stand at the door, and knock: if any man hear my voice, and open the door, I will come in to him, and will sup with him, and he with me (Revelation 3:20).

*Whosoever will may come (Revelation 22:17b).

IX

Hel-lo—

Rushing "Included—Not Excluded" Unbeliever,

I put the phone down. Have You calmed down?

YES! So, please the 4-1-1. Oh, and "please—may I—thank you!!!

(Slowly) Wel-l-l-l,

Here's the update on the Family Invitation!

GOOD...Please hurry, God! Cuz, I need to get to t-h-a-t **Par-taay!**

Dying...

*Just one notch lower on the calm down bar...please. I'll be glad to give you the information, along with the **directions** because I **really** want you there!*

*But, first let's start with a few details about how I wired Adam, your papa. He received a Family Invitation, **too**. And understanding **his** wiring will help you understand more about the Family invite.*

It's very basic: I Am Spirit. I created Adam to live on the earth—

as a spirit

who lived in a body

that had a soul

*that housed his **will***

that gave him the capacity to choose. *

Dear God,

What a nice scoop on papa's—wiring! Now, we're gettin' somewhere! This is good **INSIDE IN-FOR-MA-TION!** I'm taking notes! But, please type more slowly, God—because honestly, I really didn't realize You can type **so** fast!

D e a r D y i n g U n b e l i e v e r.

(Pardon me, God, but not **that** slowly! I'll try to keep up with our regular pace. Maybe slow down just a t-i-n-y bit.)

No problem.

Dear—Dying—Unbeliever,

(Thanks, God. That's a lot better.)

*You're welcome. Now, please let Me type **in peace!***

Yes Sir! *(smiling sheepishly, feeling a little "emboosticated!")*

You see, I Am Spirit—

Who lives in a Spiritual Realm.

but *I gave Adam a body*

to live on earth

in a natural world.

Dear God!

That sounds super major, and somewhat supernatural. And kinda important, because just like my papa, I live in a body, too!

So, does that mean—

I am **also** a spirit

who lives in a body

that has a soul

which houses my **will**

that allows me

to choose?

Yep! "Unbeliever by Choice!"

*Your **body** connects to you to the natural world—the earth.*

But Your spirit connects you to the "after-life" Spitual World—where I dwell in the Time-Zone of Eternity.

So, choose carefully while still alive on earth—humanity's "mandatory choosing station," because...

Dying Unbeliever,

*My **enemy** wants a Forever Family, too!*

But—Dear God!

Choice? What about FEELINGS?

I **f-e-e-l** like I'm already in Your Forever Family because **I f-e-e-l so close to YOU!** Certainly, my deep **feelings** of "closeness" to You suggest that I'm **already** a part of Your Family—right, God? Shouldn't my **personal f-e-e-l-ings** count for something?

In fact, I've heard that **a-l-l** souls are ALREADY Yours—! Isn't that **true,** God?

*Yep. True! **All** souls are Mine—by creation. Because I created them, but the soul that sins (refusing to return back to Me) shall die!*

*Which is why in Eternity—the eternally dead **don't** belong to Me!* It is only those who return to Me while on earth, who are My children, throughout eternity.*

So—Deep "Feeling" Unbeliever,

*Seeking to devour **all** who he can, it's the father of lies, who passes on the:*

*"I have followed my **own path**,*

*YET I **feel** close to 'God,'*

thus I am God's child theory.

*For his **best** lies start with **a heaping portion** of My truth, but are cleverly mixed in with his deadly deception. Which is why so many are led to believe that being born into this **fallen** world— **automatically** makes them the Heavenly Father's children. But the deceiver spreads the "automatic Family member" **lie** in order to gain because he wants plenty of children, too…!*

Rea-l-ly, God? Oh my! So then, **just exactly** how **can** someone become a member of **Your** Family?

*You have to be **born**-in!*

Born-in? After **already** having been born **once?** God—how? Is there a secret to solving **t-h-a-t** puzzle?

Dying Unbeliever,

It's the CROSS-WORD puzzle! He who came to the Cross solved the puzzle.

*And it is **they** who come to the Cross who **become** the Father's children.*

C

R

W ORD

S

S

Who? What? I mean—**how?**

Dying Unbeliever,

*He who was Resurrected from the **Dead** purchased your "NEW-LIFE by new-birth" Family Membership, and it's FREE.*

Invited *Unbeliever,*

Those who are born of My Spirit, and washed in the Blood—are **born-in!**

So, God—**that's** the 4-1-1?

Yep. That's the "4-1-1!"

T-h-a-t's the 4-1-WHAT?

Repeating Unbeliiever,

Is there static on the line? I didn't stutter.

The Family Invite to the "whosoever will 'Party'" was sent by the One who hung on the Cross.

And HE will accept only those whose names are covered by His blood!

Covered by His **blood!!?** Are You for real?

Dear God!

That ain't how I Party'!

And to be honest, **that ain't about to become my Party style!** So...

Dear God,

Due to reasons related to the the Blood, I respectfully decline.

Regrettably,

The Dying Unbeliever

*Behold, all souls are mine, ... (but) the soul that sinneth, it shall die (Ezekiel 18:4).

Endnotes

X

Declining while Dying...

I understand.

(Typing quietly to Himself) In a natural war, many people die—shot down by the enemy.

*In this Spiritual War, so many, sadly **choose** to refuse to return to spiritual life in Me.*

Dear God,

What made papa's war a spiritual One?

It's simple:

*Lucifer was a fallen **angel**—thus, a fallen **spirit**.*

Are not all angels ministering spirits…? (Hebrews 1:14).

I Am Spirit.

Adam is a spirit that lived in a body.

*And Satan (a fallen spirit)—through a calculated scheme—lured Adam into **his** territory of "spiritual" death.*

But, I sent My Word—a Quickening Spirit* to rescue fallen Adam. So that those enslaved to death—through him could be set FREE!

*For whom the **SON** sets free is free, **indeed!***

Tell me it AIN'T SO, God! Tell me my papa ***didn't*** become a **slave**** in that **bloody** War?

Yep! Enslaved Unbeliever who rejects the freeing bloody Cross! He did!

Oh no!!! Captured papa—ended up on the slave block!!!

Oh, dear!

*Endnotes

XI

Dear God!

I didn't realize papa's circumstances were so bleak.

So now, I'm a lot more concerned about my dear ole' dad's dying conditions. Since taken captive in a **Spiritual** War, what happened to his **physical** body?

Well, Dying Unbeliever,

As a casualty of the War, Adam's spirit died immediately! But his body continued living and breathing temporarily until it finally quit. In other words, after his fall, the "earthen" part of Adam lived on—but died gradually—due to the death process that sin released in him, until he finally departed the earth.

Alive physically, but dead spiritually—b-o-t-h at the **same** time, God?

But wouldn't that make life **hard?**

Oh, very hard, Dying Unbeliever. And it robs from the sum of "total life." Basically—it's just bad math!

One *living body*

minus one living spirit

plus one broken soul

equaled a TOTAL disaster for Adam!

Dear God!

SO, fallen papa ALSO **flunked math?**

Dying Unbeliever,

*Absolutely **no-thing** added up!*

Who-a-a! Good thing **I'm not flunken' "life" math—TOO!**

Dear "Life"-Flunken' and Disconnected from Me" Unbeliever!

"Listen Adam," I warned, "Leave that forbidden fruit tree alone. Because, in the <u>same</u> day that you eat from it, you will surely die!"

Dear God!!!

Papa **flunked** listening, <u>too</u>?

*Nope. **Listening** Unbeliever,*

*Adam **listened** just fine, but he FAILED to obey MY WORD!*

***But** despite his failure to obey—My Word **still** NEVER fails!!*

XII

〰️

"Flunken'" disconnected **foolishness…**Goodness Gracious! Can there be more than a **"fixation on the fallen"** around here?

Dear God,

I'm not trying to be mean, but I don't know if You noticed that it looks like Your score in math is looking kinda low—**too**. No disrespect intended—but the numbers that came after "the 'same day' death warning" You gave to papa didn't *quite* add up—**ei-ther**.

Oh, really?

How do you figure?

Well God,

Here's my facts: After reviewing our last email thread, I see that You warned my papa, that in the <u>"SAME"</u> day that he ate from that tree, he would **"surely die."** But, in an earlier statement, You wrote something contradictory.

Type on! Fact-Finding Unbeliever—Type on!

With pleasure! Case in point, You indicated that while my papa's sprit died **immediately,** "...*his body continued living and breathing temporarily until it finally quit*!" (NOTE: **Exact** words.)

So—since papa **kept living physically** day-after-day-after-day, **even a-f-ter** he got a taste of that "deadly" fruit, it looks like despite **Your clear** warning, my papa **did not "surely"** die on the **same** day of his misstep, when he fell!

So-o-o—God (feeling self-important and quite pleased),

I drop the mic!!

SIDE NOTE: For clarification, God. Down here "a mic drop" is the way we display our **bold** confidence that the point we just made is extremely impressive and can't be topped!

Oh—and here's just one final point, God, SO sorry, but You might want to check Your **Word,** as well! Kinda looks like the Word You Spoke didn't quite pan out on Your "same day... death warning," **either**. Basically—**despite** Your cautioning papa that on the **s-a-m-e** day that he ate of that bad fruit, he would "surely" die—w-el-l-l, he did "eat," b-u-t kept **right on living a l-o-n-g t-i-m-e**—!

(Smugly) Now! I'll respectfully accept Your response!

Well... Well... Well "Math and Word-Checking" Unbeliever!

*So, you've found a problem with My math calculations **and** MY Word—huh?*

Yes Sir! God!

Oh, and just **one** small request: I know You're still the Boss, but to be fair to gracefully accepting constructive criticism, may I count on You to double-check **both** your math **and** Your Word, going forward!--?

We-e-l-l-l Let's See,

*To be fair to gracefully accepting a **failed** mic drop—may I count on you to both pick up **and** put up your mic RIGHT NOW!*

Investigatve Unbeliever With an "Earth-Only" View!

*My Word **never** fails, and My math is **never** off! If I SAY—the **same** day, it means the **same** day!*

So, pay attention, "Dying Mic" Dropper!

I'll explain!

*There are **so** many who take your stance. When viewing the affairs of My earth, some attempt to dismiss My interaction in its earthly equations.*

It can't work!

*There are TWO sides to humanity's reality…the natural side **and** the spiritual side. Not only earth, but heaven must be factored in when doing life calculations.*

*For example, in matters of the blood, there are **both** sides. So I factor in not only the biological, but ALSO the spiritual construct of "blood" matters. Case in point: Adam's bloodline. I placed biological life in Adam's blood,* for the blood deposit I gave to him was for the purpose of physical life transactions. But his rebellion contaminated his life/blood with sin—and ultimately caused his separation from Me—"a spiritual transaction".*

*Under the dual biological and spiritual lens of My microscope, I not only observe matters of humanity's biological blood (Blood Types A, B, AB, O). **But I also** see and hear the matters of each individual's spiritual blood condition (either "cleansed" or still contaminated with Adam's highly contagious sin-virus.) For example, "I heard the blood of Abel cry out to Me for **JUDGEMENT** when he died—**killed by** angry Cain, his brother, in a jealous fit of rage. **Before long**—I ALSO heard the Cleansing Blood of My Son cry out to Me for—**MERCY*** when he died—**killed** by those who He came to Redeem.*

*Humanity's attempts to diminish or dismiss Me are laughable. For conclusions drawn that "disprove God" are drawn by those who view life **only** through the lens of the affairs of the earth. But the failure to factor in the "spiritual" component of MY creation is only foolery, and it is the fool who says in his heart, says there is NO God—.* For I handle the affairs of heaven and earth, good and evil, life and death, and Satan reports to Me.**

I gave humanity 20/20 vision, but as the Creator, I possess HEAVEN/EARTH vision to behold ALL things. And only those among humanity who look through the lens of faith—see Me. Faith is the substance of things hoped for, and the evidence of things not seen.* And without faith, it is impossible to please

Me,* because those who come to Me on earth, must believe without seeing. But My people WILL see Me, one day.

I Am GOD.

As in matters of time,

*I see time in **both** earth's **and** heaven's time systems.*

Which is why you did not understand My Time Calculations with Adam,

On "Earth's-Time" Calculator!

*—**one day is as a 1000 years with Me—God.****

So…regarding My "same" day warning to Adam…

I did the math on My end, according to MY Eternal calculations.

With Me—

***One** earth day period (24 hours)*

*is as **1000** years in "God" Day calculations.*

*Thus, **1000** years on My Eternal Calendar*

*is the equivalent of **one** full earth-day.*

*And **none** among Adam's universal family*

has <u>ever</u> lived to reach the full age of

1000 years (One Eternal Day)—

Thus, calculations show that

*no human has **ever** lived **one** full "God" Day—on earth*

in "God" Day calculations

based on MY Calendar!

*Therefore, Adam **did** die*

*the **same** day of his transgression…*

*…in **My** Time System*

*and according to **My** Eternal Calendar.*

As humanity's Creator

…My Time

always Counts.

Well, God—I guess I can see that!

But wait,

Are you suggesting that You have a calendar?

Yep! And a calculator, too!

And on that note, let Me point this out, in closing:

Despite Adam's sudden "spirit-death" experience, I needed Adam's family to remain alive physically on the earth to help complete My Divine Purpose! And I gave humanity dominion over My earth, through Adam For those who will **return** back to life in Me will do a great work in the earth. We will walk together—work together—My people will worship Me—and I will bless them—and we will love, like family—**for My people are My heritage, which is My greatest treasure!***

And according to My calculations—MANY will be born into My Forever Family! And they shall be MINE!

D-E-A-R GOD!!!

*Was that an **EARTHQUAKE???!!!!!***

*Yep! I just dropped **MY Mic!***

*Endnotes

XIII

[The **Shaken** Unbeliever types quietly with a new tone of "after-earth-quake" God-respect and humility.]

But God,

It sounds like it was ALL my papa's fault for messing up Your Plan.

Dying Unbeliever,

"Freedom of choice" is definitely risky business, and Adam proved the point, well. Yep. His forbidden tree experience was something we both felt, but I ALWAYS have a back-up Plan!

[*Too quickly recovered from the voice of heightened respect, Dying returns back to a testy tone.*]

Plans! Plans! Rubber Bands! It's crystal clear! Papa shouldah practiced **"safe selection"**—(in fruit-tree options.)

And by the way, God!

Exactly **what t-y-p-e** of fruit was that tree growin'? And since it caused **SO** much trouble, why was that problem tree PLANTED in that Garden in the first place...just **so** unnecessary!

*Oh, it was **quite** necessary, Irritated Unbeliever!*

The forbidden tree produced the forbidden fruit that would introduce Adam to evil, if ever consumed.

*And because of the Two Eternal Options available—life **or** death—it was **mandatory** that Adam—have access to not only the tree of life, but **also** to the forbidden tree choice that leads to death!*

Su-per-Blooper!!! GOD!

TREE OF LIFE? What? You mean papa could've chosen **L-I-F-E,** instead of **death?**

*Yep. But the deceiver is **crafty, conniving and "luringly" skillful** in his capturing tactics.*

Good grief! **Careless** papa!

Much Grief, careless Unbeliever!

Adam got captured—bound—and Warden Satan was delighted when he gained eternal possession of Adam through eternal death and the grave!

Delighted?

But why, God? What delight was there in papa's **captivity?**

Bound in captivity Unbeliever,

Eternal misery LOVES eternal company!

And when captive humanity started falling into Satan's eternal prison one by one—the warden—was ECSTATIC!!!

Ecstatic over people being shackled in chains? That can't be good for guaranteed Constitutional freedom. What about human rights? So, what's the back-up plan, God? Is there **Anyone** who can UNLOCK GRIPPING locks and chains?

Well, Locked and Chained Unbeliever.

It would have to be the Chain-Breaker!

Dear God!

My papa was the leader of a Chain Gang?

Good Grief! ADAM and MADAM!

Now everybody needs a Locksmith to be freed!

OH~MY!!!

XIV

Top of the Morning to You, God.

Been thinkin'. Was there ANY way Big Papa could've just escaped—broken out?

Gettin' a death sentence for bad fruit consumption, would make ANYONE want to **be set free!**

Not possible, Dying Unbeliever!

*Adam was a powerless Prisoner of War, and there was **no** way he could break himself free.*

Yuck! Yuck!

Stucky—stuck!!!

Dear God,

Papa's "bad fruit" penalty was quite A LOT stiffer than today's basic sentence for eatin' wilted grapes, too many prunes, or a rotten banana—which can be MULTIPLE trips to the rest-stop—at an awkward time. Now, t-h-a-t rumble can make you **literally** run!

Okay—that'll be enough of the update on an upset digestive system—"Sour Stomach" Unbeleiver!!!

(Buurrp) Excuse me—God. So, then where was I? Oh yes. If I see this correctly, papa's plight left him pretty much STUCK—up a **fruit tree** without a paddle!

VERY MUCH so!

*So it would have to be Someone Who holds Infinite Power over Death's Choke Hold—willing to Die on a "life-forgiving" **tree**— Who could lift Adam UP and bring humanity OUT!*

Dear God,

A Super-Power "life-loser" dying on a tree—? Is there ANYONE who would do THAT? I just don't **think** so!

(Clearly, has heard enough) Dying Unbeliever,

*But do you **think** you can **stop** mixing your metaphors! It's "up **the river** without a paddle"—not up **a fruit tree!***

I'm sorry, God. The tree is a sensitive topic for you—isn't it?

…but let me explain. I said, "up a fruit tree without a paddle," accidently because I can't stop thinking about that **"booby-trap of death,"** disguised as a fruit tree—that resulted in poor papa **sinking his teeth into such "hot trouble!"**

He should've left that FORSTINKIN' fruit tree alone! You would think a universal dad would've known if you play with **a "hot fruit tree," eventually you're gonna get burned! AND if the heat is too hot, GET OUT the garden!**

Good Lord!

"Hot tree" papa threw the family under the bus!

"Hot Talkin'" Unbeliever...

Who-o-a there! Sl-o-w-w-w down!

*The tree was "forbidden," not **"forstinkin,"** and it's **fire** that burns! And "if the heat is too hot, get out the kitchen"—NOT the **garden!!***

*PLEEEASE get **y-o-u-r** words straight—Confused Unbeliever! Especially since You questioned **Mine!***

[Mildly sarcastic] Oh, that felt great! I didn't know questioning Your Word would upset You **that** much, God.

*Always does! That's JUST what happened in the Garden. My Word was not accepted, **as Truth**—and I Honor My Word above My Name!!!**

[The Typing Unbeliever does not pay attention to "God's" Truth, but keeps right on typing about Adam's woes.]

...and because of **universal papa** now **everybody** has to live in a WORLD of The Big Three! Debt—Death, and Destruction!

Good grief!

"Hot-fruit" papa!

FORSHAME FORKILLIN' the FAMILY DREAM!

*For thou hast magnified thy word above all thy name (Psalm 138:2).

XV

Hold it! "Papa-Shaming" Unbeliever,

*Have you **no** empathy for your universal **dad?***

True. Adam fell into a problem…

But it was one that is common to A-L-L humanity.

He was self-willed,

—bit into a tasty,

but forbidden experience

—got trapped

and discovered, with tears,

*that he was **no** match*

for the master of alluring deception.

But, God. I just **can't** excuse my papa's behavior!

In fact, I've been doing a lota thinkin'!

I might have **some** of Adam's faults and traits, but here's where I'm **completely** different from fallen papa!

I don't have a rebellious bent. And, **I** f-e-e-l fairly unstained. And God—**I've never** gone out on a "forbidden-fruit" tasting binge a day in **my** life!

So, spiritually—? Basically, **I'm** o-k-a-y. **A-n-d!** As a 21st Century "free-spirit," I doubt that "forever-death" is really applicable to me! Not bragging, God, but **MY** "earth" path experience has been **almost** flawless! I have a great track record…not perfect, but definitely "evolving," and in a good space—overall.

That said! I don't think I really need to **ever** worry about **all** that EDS stuff, like broken papa.

EDS?

Oh! Yes, God!

It's a short texting phrase for "Extreme Death Scare!" And, by the way…I've noted that that seems to be **SUCH** a major theme of Your emailing!

So, btw (by the way) God,

Do You believe in reincarnation? I mean folks dying, and then coming back to an "after-life" experience in some specific form for a second time around (—**and maybe even beyond**—) to avoid being stuck in the grave?

Nope. Dying Unbeliever. But btw—,

*Do you believe in "Resurrection?" I mean My folks rising UP— to avoid being stuck in the grave when the **alarm** goes off, and it's time to wake up from **the dead?***

(Disinterested) Dear God,

So—I guess You would say, "to escape **a D-J-E"?**

A D-J what?

Oh—that would be a "Downer Judgement Experience!"

Sorry, God, but **that's** where we differ! As a 21st Century enlightened thinker who does not subscribe to the bias that seems to define the narrowness of Your **"judging"** style—**I choose** to refuse **any** idea that is unaccepting of an *opposing point of view!*

AND so...sorry for my oppositional position against Your "Word!" But de-s-pite Your perspective—my spirit feels like it's set to soar "resurrection-style," with or without a "Blood" Transfusion from Your Son. In fact—inside, I f-e-e-l totally free.

Like—"AMAZING Spirit-freedom" for days!

So, **eternal** death? Don't see it comin'! And to be perfectly honest, the basic "spirit-death" concept seems fairly **old-fashioned** to me.

So counter to what You might've intended, our conversation has done wonders to remind me of how SPIRIT ALIVE I **r-e-a-l-y** AM—and how highly e-v-o-l-v-e-d I'M **becoming!**

Sorry, God—not to be down-right cocky! But (ijs) I'm just sayin'!

Endnotes

XVI

*Dear "Alive and Free Spirit" 21ˢᵗ Century Highly Evolved **y-e-t** Dying Unbeliever!*

Yep!

*You and I agree on o-n-e point, **completely!***

*In fact, "Eternal Death by Family Affiliation" IS much more than **old-fashioned.** It's down-right ancient! Started thousands of years ago!*

But God! I wasn't referring **to t-h-a-t!** In fact, I don't think I've **ever** heard of such a thing 'til I started talking to You! Eternal Death by Family Affiliation?

Dying Unbeliever!

Yep!

Through one Adamic birth at a time!

Really, God? Seriously? Are You suggesting my connection to "Adam's sin" is **REALLY** why I'M facing death **all-l-l these years** LATER?

It is.

And, so God—You're actually saying that through Adam's contaminated blood-line, somehow "Adam's sin" R-E-A-L-L-Y got on me?

Dying Unbeliever—It did!

And, I'm sorry to notify you, but as one of Adam's kin—there's yet <u>another</u> layer to your dilemma!

Another layer? **Not MORE! Death?** God—Please!

[God Silence]

Dear God,

Break the news gently**!**

MERCY A little **mer-cy!** What is it, God?

Desperate since Dying Unbeliever,

*When Adam's spirit was cut off from the life of My Spirit that had once kept **h-i-s spirit eternally** alive—*

NO! Please, don't tell me! Because **YOUR** "spirit-life" oxygen was cut-off in **papa**—I was born with a chronic case of **COSOS?**

COSOS???

YES!!! CUT-OFF "**Spirit-life**" Oxygen SYNDROME!

God—Please let it not be so!

This is **QUITE** unbearable!

Dear Carrier of the Chronic COSOS Gene,

(Gasping for air and voice trembling) Y~e~s, God?

I'm breaking it to you as gently as I can!

When sin and death unplugged Adam from life in Me...

(Interrupts) No, God! Please DON'T say it! That means **I** was born spiritually **UNPLUGGED**—too...? And because of **papa's** disconnection, now there's **NO** spirit-life oxygen flowing to **me~e?**

Pretty please—GOD!!! Mercy.

So, You're telling Me—**I ca~n't breathe~e~e?**

Not spiritually—through MY Life! Disconnected—, Unbeliever!

NO oxygen **at all? A~I~R! Please, A~I~R!**

Despite our oxygen differences, God. EVERYBODY deserves a strong ox~y~gen FLO~~W.

Gasping Unbeliever!

*In Adam, there is no FLOW. It's been **Totally** Terminated!!! Which is why you've been so desperately connecting to "spiritual-life oxygen substitutes"—that are outside of the life that can ONLY flow from Me—!*

But God~~~, **I was on~ly trying to bre~e~eathe!**

A good "life-oxygen" **substitute** should—**(Deeply gasping)** H~E~l~p...n~o, God?

Spirit-lifeless Unbeliever,

Nope!

—***any*** *"spiritual-substitute-life source" that does not flow from the Power of My "life-giving" Spirit is an empty source that will lead to...*

Eternal Suffo-cation due to severe spi-ri-tual AIR flow de-pri-va-tion?

God, can You check my HeArT?

(Deep sin-virus cough) So does that mean that because of papa's fall, **I** was **born** with a **serious** case of the "Be-yond-bea-se?"

The Beyondbease?

Y-es God. **The Beyond Broken Spiritual Lung Dis-ease!!!**

God, this is **hard**!

Yes—Severe Beyondbease Sufferer.

Adam's fall was hard on Me, too!

So God...since my papa lost **his** breath—does it mean, **I'm spi-ritual-ly** breathl-e-s-s, **too?**

*Sorry to break it to you... Spiritually Breathless Unbeliever, **cut-off** from Me! But—Yep.*

S-o-oo—HARD God! And a-ll the time I've been liven', my spirit has <u>N-E-V-E-R</u> breathed ANY of Your FRESH Spirit a-i-r?-

*Nope! 'Fraid not, "Spirit-**Airless**" Unbeliever!*

Dear God. **No~o~o** I'm GASP~I~N~G!

God! Please. ONE Breath~I need some SPIRITUAL AIR! **N~O~W!!!**

This is **serious**—would this mean **I'm spir~it~ually de~ceased?**

Dying Unbeliever! I know this is hard!

So hard, God—**I'm spi~ri~tually DEAD!!?**

Dying Unbeliever!

It's been that way for years.

(Completely startled. Sits up erect to gain a breath.)

Y-E-A-R-S???

I NEED—HELP! I CAN'T B-R-E-A-T-H-E! **[THUD!!!]**

[The Dying Unbeliever falls to the floor, and makes a LOUD thud before frantically gasping for air.]

DEAR GOD!!

HE-L-LP! I'M SPIRITUALLY FALLEN AND I CAN'T GET UP!

It's my heart! I GOT A B-A-D HEART!!!

Dying Unbeliever,

***QUIET down!** You'll wake up this **whole** hospital!*

I'm calm! [Climbs back in bed]

Pl-ease cooperate, God!

Get the spiritual paramedics. I need **spiritual CPR! Please R-E-S-I-S-T ANY delay!!!** God—PLEASE!!! FIND **somebody!** ANYBODY who can administer **spirit-life resuscitation!**

I CAN'T BREATHE-E-E!

Dying Unbeliever!

***HE ALREADY CAME,** but <u>you've</u> **refused** to PLUG-IN!*

Who came? **You mean the Man who <u>hung</u> on a tree? Oh, no! Thanks! But—I don't do blood!**

So—NE-X-XT!

[The Dying Unbeliever "THUDS" to the floor again.]

Okay! You're done!

Now, look **DRA-MA-TIC** *Thudder! GET UP, RIGHT NOW!*

I've **never** *had high blood pressure, and I don't intend to get it—so I don't want to experience that* **EVER** *again!*

You just SLAMMED yourself on to the floor…TWICE, **and almost broke your LEG AND your computer!** *And guess who You'll want to* **FIX every—thing?** *M-E!!*

So, listen here, little Unbeliever!

Get up!

Get back in that hospital bed!

And go to sleep—RIGHT THIS SECOND! By the time I get to 5, you'd better be FAST asleep!

1, 2, 3, 4!

Lights out, God!

I'm snoring…

Z-z-z-z-z-z-z-z-z-z **Z-Z-Z-Z-Z…**z

z

z.

XVII

[Yawning and stretching out of sleep.]

Sorry, God for all the drama!

I didn't expect to go **tha-at** far out of character.

But papa just **blew it!**

Dying Unbeliever,

Yes, he did!

And God…

The mess he made was **BIG**! And now because of papa's carelessness, I've contracted a **bad** case of the SBC virus!

Yes, you do have quite a case—SBCver.

(To the "Newly Acknowledging" Support Group "NA")

And acknowledging this has been <u>somewhat</u> difficult, but "I am the Dying Unbeliever—a chronic SBCver, and I am a (hesitating to collect courage)… 24/7 Sinful Blood Contamination Virus carrier—and **it's killing me! There's even been times when I've committed up to three sins a day!**

(Group) **"Hi,** Dyin'"

Thank you. I just hope there's a cure.

"Newly Acknowledging" Unbeliever,

*There **is** a cure!*

In My Eternal Steps for the SBCver Manual—

You will find that

*the fight Adam **could** have undertaken at the tree…*

*is the **same** fight that those addicted to sin*

***can** put up today!*

It's the

Same enemy!

Same scheme!

Same defense!

*Receive **My Word.***

*Obey **My Word!***

***Submit** to God!**

Resist the devil!

And you can be set free!

Your Word?

My Son!

But—dear God?

Resist?

What about **Co-exist?**

I've always been told that in matters of spirituality, humanity should co-exist, and be respectful of a different god!

Dying Unbeliever,

*That's what **Adam tried!***

But—papa **failed THAT experiment.**

Yep. And humanity's been fighting death's addictions—misery and afflictions to this day!

Oh…dear! I'm gonna leave the meeting early. *Excuse me!!!*

*Submit yourselves therefore to God. Resist the devil, and he will flee from you. James 4:7

XVIII

Dear God,

[After several minutes, no response.]

God,

Are You there?

Yes, Dying Unbeliever. I was dealing with a matter with a few of the angels.

Is everything okay?

All's well. They just got back from an emergency intervention to help fix a problem in the earth. Along with Archangel Michael, they helped turn "defeat into victory" in a situation, and were sharing the pictures with Me.

Nice shots, God?

Excellent! There's lots of talent in that group. Now, what's on your mind?

Well, God. I've been thinking. Since I got a pretty bad blood stain from papa, can You recommend something that can take it out?

Yep. A good cleansing "B" Bath will completely remove Adam's stain.

Thanks, God!

I just knew You would have the answer! A good "B"ubble Bath to wash away papa's filth is such a totally RELAXING idea!!

A bubble bath?

Nope.

"Relaxing" Unbeliever!

*It's THE **"B"** Bath. That's why My Son, the Second Adam, got involved. He was the only Other Man beside the first Adam, who I sent to the earth with unstained, non-contaminated blood! He came to help…*

…my papa?

Yep! Because I knew My Son could keep His allotment of pure "life-giving" blood refreshingly clean!

And, He did.

*So, as—the Unblemished One—He made a sacrificial contribution to humanity. He gave the **only** Cleansing Agent available that can wash away Adam's stain!*

It's a "Blood Bath" that you need, Unwashed Unbeliever. It's heaven's "Liquid Wash Detergent," and it will leave you refreshed, and "amazing-grace spirit-life connected" clean!

A blood bath?

Not gonna happen! Didn't we get passed that? I've **always** been taught NOT to allow A-N-Y-B-O-D-Y'S blood to get on me

See—God,

It's gloves, masks, soap and the whole shabang. That's what ALL major hospitals on earth require for the proper handling of blood—cautions ALL supported by researched. A-n-d, "life-saving" blood can ONLY be handled by someone who is properly certified!

So—not to be overly critical, but that's just **one** of the short-comings of Your Son's blood. There's absolutely NO scientific research out there to substantiate the **high** effectiveness of His "cleansing blood" claim. Also, there's no documentation on earth's records that show that He's Heart Association **Board Certified** to give "spiritual-life" Blood Transfusions.

Dear Sin-Certified Unbeliever,

*The eternal effectiveness of My Son's blood **transcends** human research and scientific logic! It has been tested in the laboratory of heaven, and is approved by the HRB!*

Ummm—the HRB, God?

Yep. The Heavenly Review Board for Cleansing Blood Research, of which I Am the Department Chair. As the One who Co-designed the creation of Pure Blood with Me, My ONLY begotten Son— as the ONLY qualified Man—serves on the Board, and holds a vested interest in Operation ABCP.

Operation ***ABCP***, God?

Yep—Adam's Blood Cleansing Project.

The HRB determined that My Son's blood type is the <u>only</u> blood type that is compatible with My Paternal pure righteousness, the life of My Spirit, AND Adam's original deposit of pure blood. Humanity's spiritual need for uncorrupted blood is one of the main reasons My Son came to earth.

When My Son's "life-blood" is willingly applied by the Sinful Blood Contamination Virus carrier, the SBCver is able to meet humanity's Move-in Regulations into My Home—as ENFORCED by My Son.

Enforced by **Your Son?**

Yep. My Son. After He went to the earth and returned from work, I put Him in charge of Operation Move-in for humanity's cleansed entrance into My Estate.

So, exactly what **are** Your "Move-in Regulations," God?

It's very basic. ALL applicants MUST first apply the blood to be sin-stained, and "enemy-stench" free.

XIX

Dear God,

I think it's time for Me to be completely honest about this matter of the blood!

Number 1

I'm pretty sure not **everybody's** going to want to apply it!

Number 2

According to Federal Fair Housing Discrimination Policies, listing Your Son's blood as a move-in requirement to gain access into heaven's property, likely places You in violation of a Federal Fair Housing Law.

Earth's Government has a comprehensive book of Federal Guidelines, and God, I'm not trying to tell You how to govern Your Property, but **down here** housing discrimination is a serious violation.

Dear Dying Unbeliever,

*My House is **UP** Here!*

And it operates s-t-r-i-c-t-l-y under the Eternal Fair Housing Jurisdiction, which operates by MY policies—according to MY Government Guidelines.

*Thus, the requirement for My Son's cleansing blood to be applied, before a member of **fallen** humanity can gain entrance into My Propery, is fair and binding. It will not be rescinded for the following Cross related decision—separated into Three Parts—as listed in MY Comprehensive Book of Eternal Guidelines:*

Cross Decision #1

My Son willingly shed life-cleaning blood.

Cross Decision #2

It's Powerful, Plentiful, and available to ALL!

Cross Decision #3 It's Free, Flowing, and Freeing!, and leads to Spirit-Life Connection!

*And to avoid ANY confusion, I will make this Eternally Clear! "My Eternal Life Guarantee," as set forth in My Written Word— is conditional on humanity's FULL implementation of MY specified guidelines. It is not contingent upon humanity's **acceptance of, or agreement with** ANY of My Terms, as clearly indicated in writing. (Refer to My Life-Giving Manual.)*

*As the Only Wise God—My expectation as Creator, is that humanity will enter into **full** compliance with My Laws—as set forth in the Book—which I sent to the earth for humanity's Instruction and Guidance.*

*Governed by My Sovereign Authority, I will **not** alter or rescind ANY of My statements.*

For individuals who are out of compliance with My Will, the Confession/Forgiveness Clause, as established by My Word, through the work of My Son on Calvary, is what I have put into effect.

*To start or restore acceptable standing by **ANYONE** who stands opposed to Me—the opposing party must establish **FULL-immediate** alignment with My Word.*

*Do not **add to or subtract from** My Book! For the misrepresentation of My Word is a deadly offense to Me.*

For My children: A side note reminder. Your body is the temple of God. So, keep My temple pure, for My Holy Spirit is housed within you

As God the Father

My Plan for for humanity's redemption was Executed in FULL by My Son, Empowered by the Quickening Force of My Spirit! And I AM the Head of ALL!!!

Those in Heaven and Earth, and those Under the Earth do MY Bidding.

*Each will live or die eternally—in accordance with **the Governance of My Ruling Power**—as spoken by **My Eternal Word.***

This Edict has been Established on this Day by The Council of My Sovereign Will:

Signed in Agreement by the Triune Community of One:

God the Father

God the Son

God the Holy Spirit

Written in the Blood of My Eternal Heir.

(Thundering silence…unable to think of a response.)

(Inserts foot in mouth.) Dear God,

That was really passionate. I would think most people would want to be in agreement with **You.** But, in all honesty, it's Your Son who seems to create the resistance!

In fact, I'm thinking it's the "Blood-Bath" regulation clause that probably explains why His numbers are so low.

(Doesn't know when to stop.) **"Willfully"** washing with ANYBODY's blood is **risky,** and **really** an unattractive offer! And quite frankly, I'm not WILLING to touch it.

So, many thanks, God! But I'll pass! I'm good.

XX

Good?

Dying Unbeliever,

*Nope. **Not good!***

*You wouldn't know it, but My House holds the "Eternal Good Housekeeping Award!" It's a **very** prestigious honor, which acknowledges the cleanliness and beauty of My Home, along with the purity of its occupants! Most importantly, it's My SON'S work that protects this prestigious honor of My Estate.*

Dear God,

I can tell Your Son is a hard worker, and clearly has some high points! *And, congrats on Your Award! But I do have to be honest, Your Son is a VERY controversial Figure down here. And not to be mean, but a huge fault with Him is that He's **super one-sided** about His personal views.*

Wel-l-l, "One-Sided" Unbeliever.

And for good reason! After Lucifer started his "death" rebellion in My House, My Son wanted to insure that Our Property would remain a "Rebellion and Death-Free Zone," going forward.

*He knows, I want a Family, but that I **can't stand** the odor of sin, rebellion, and death—and I don't want another WAR up here, so He really went out the way to secure the House! The Cross was the answer! It made a **BIG** difference because now humanity can move-in, but **must** first clear a Top-Security "Bloodwashed" check.*

Blood-Infected Unbeliever,

*I **HUGELY** appreciate My Son because had He not finished His work on earth, the **only** residents allowed in My Home would be the loyal angels. None among infected-fallen humanity could have come to Me because carriers of the active death contaminent must be eternally quarantined to its originating source.*

But—why, God? Why wouldn't You have wanted it just like that? **ONLY** angels? If only angels lived in my house, there would be a lot fewer problems, I'm sure! I'm thinking it's the people who bring the drama!!

Loved Unbeliever,

Angels are wonderful. They're My warriors and servants, and while I deeply appreciate heaven's angels, humanity has My Heart.

Reea-ly God,

But—why?

So-Loved One,

*Because when My Son would rescue Adam—**then,** Adam would become My son—by choice.*

XXI

*You see…the angels were created to **worship** Me.*

*But humanity was created to **choose** to worship Me.*

What's the difference, God? That like sounds like such a **minor** difference.

Unbeliever Created to Choose!

*Oh, no—there's nothing minor in **that!***

Here's the difference:

When I created Lucifer and the angels, I was the ONLY God.

There was no other God for the angels to choose to worship, besides Me. For, the Creator is due proper acknowledgement.

But Lucifer, exploiting the high-ranking power I gave him as a leading angel, exalted himself, attempting to rise to My Throne. With "self-exalting" worship, he influenced a third of My angels to worship him. In this sinful deed of pride, He became, the *"alternative" god who created the option for angels, and eventually humanity, to choose **whom** to worship?*

God or god?

*So, Lucifer's "self-exalted fall" was his introduction to the concept of **another** god attempting to sit on My Throne, as Lord of All.*

Consequently, with the Sovereign God/fallen god option in place—I created Adam and his family—to choose?*

But God,

Why do You require so much worship?

Magnificently Created Unbeliever,

*The Creator who created such a **magnificent** creation is due honor from His handiwork. I Am a loving, gracious God—Who is the giver of ALL life. I gave both My angels and Adam a generous portion of life and godliness*—as the life-giving Creator— and for that reason, I Am worthy to be Honored and Glorified, for Life.*

But, you see, Dying Unbeliever,

*Satan, resents that. So, in rebellion—he made **himself** a god.*

*—a **lesser** god.*

*—a **fallen** god.*

*—a **false** god.*

*With a false voice of deception that still **despises** MY WORD, and still deceives—today*

For he—too—wants to expand his "family," ** and does so through the masterful, cunning deception of misleading lies— Misled Unbeliever.

XXII

And speaking of family—Back to My Son!

After Lucifer's Rebellion, We BOTH decided, I'm TOO OLD for ANY MORE drama coming to the House! So my enemy's folks have to stay away!!!

In fact, My Son said, ANYBODY who wants to come to Me, has to go through HIM FIRST!

Then He reared back and said, "Dad... I rolled up on death, stomped on the devil's head—and M-A-D-E MY POINT! I wasn't playing!!!

WOW God!

Your Son sounds kinda **Gangsta!**

Dying Unbeliever,

*Watch **that** slang!*

But you know, Dying...

There might be something to that! I was somewhat surprised Myself when He returned Home from the earth and **started** *talking like THAT!*

(God speaks quietly to Himself.) Yep. He learned that "kinda" talk from His mother's side! She knew, coming from Heaven to a new neighborhood, He would have to be tough!!!

In fact, as soon as He got back to the House, He posted a sign on the gate that reads:

"Come clean or stay away dirty!"

His exact Words...

"Father, I gave **cleansing** *blood!"*

And then He showed Me His nail-scarred hands.

Now He's telling Me that He's packing His bags to go back down to take over the earth, one day!* He's not happy at all about how Satan's tryng to take over!!!*

I'll tell you the truth,

Dying Unbeliever,

I'm **NOT going to be the One** *to get in His Way! Because, I know My Son. When HE talks like that—He* **MEANS** *BUSINESS! Well, I must admit—He got His talking about returning to the earth to take over from—listening to Me!!! So, it looks like He got some of His...*

(Excitedly interrupting) **...SMACK** talkin', GOD!!

(Hesitantly) ...well, "Smack talkin'" from Me—! To tell the truth—having a Son who started out as God, and then got wrapped up in Human Flesh is really something else! In fact, one night, just outta nowhere—He looked up from the earth and said, "Look dad, I'm walking on water!"* It was a "creation treat" to watch Him make Our contrary ocean and wind behave—the ocean and wind He created, as My Word! I was moved!!! Yep. It takes quite a Man to carry MY Power—and He Nailed IT, before getting nailed f-o-r it! But, He'd use that **s-a-m-e** "ocean-commanding" Power to empty His grave, **beatin' My enemy down!!!** with His DADDY'S PUNCH!!! (Umm, Looks I'm doin' a little "Smack" talkin'—Myself!!! But the way My Son **handled HIS Busi-n-e-s-s** with RESURRECTION POWER made Me **go t-h-e-r-e!**)

(Returns to calm speaking) Having become such a fine Combination of the Heaven/Earth Man—He's going to make an EXCELLENT Ruler of My Earth, one day—ruling and reigning as Sovereign King—with My Power!!!

Walkin' on water—? KING? Wow, God!

Gangsta for sho!!!

"Slang-Talkin'" Unbeliever,

Watch that slang!

Oh 'xcuse Me God—It slipped (just like papa)!

*Endnotes

XXIII

Speaking of slippin' 'cuz of sin... I been meaning to ask you, God.

Just, exactly **how** repulsive is sin to You?

Dying Unbeliever,

*Just <u>imagine</u> someone offering you a completely **filthy** cup of water.*

Okay,

But—do You mean, to drink?

*Yes, and to the **last** drop!*

Dear God,

Just <u>imagine</u> a HUGE cup of yuck! That would be completely **disgusting!**

So God, just out of curiosity, what **ingredients** would be in the **"filthy"** cup?

Well—Curious Unbeliever,

Let's see? Imagine a few dead flies, poison, and virus germs, all served in an unwashed cup, laced with disease and rotting infection.

*It's your choice!!! Would you **accept it** and want to **drink it completely?***

No-o-o way, God!

Because that would be a ***drink creeply!***

So, what kind of a qu-es-tion is that, anyway? I don't think there's **ANYBODY** within a MILLION miles who would accept that filth! I'd straight **r-e-f-u-s-e it!**

Dying Unbeliever,

*Just as I **refuse** the filth of Sin!*

*Which is why humanity's **sinful** rebellion...self-will...wicked-ness...deception...and lustful pride are **repulsive** to Me.*

Many attempt to offer Me that kind of garbage from the "cups" of their unwashed lives, and I will not...

… drink it?

I will not, Dying Unbeliever!

So My Son's "blood-purifying" treatment purifies the water of humanity back to its original refreshing state!

Because—Unclean Unbeliever,

He knows how much I so enjoy connecting with a refreshing-ly-cleansed life made clean through His purifying work!!

(Kindly connecting) Dear God,

I have a water purifier.

Then, you know how wonderfully satisfying clean fresh water can be!

Dear God,

Only somewhat! I'm more of a **"bubbly-fiz soda"** kind of unbeliever! But the doctor said I have to start drinking more water.

B-O-R-I-N-G!

*"Bubbly with **Sugar**,"*

Drink that water!

Okay, God, but don't be surprised if You don't hear me yell **"Yuck"** super loud!

Bubbly—with Drama,

Trust Me—I won't be surprised at all!

*After your fainting spell, and your **very** dramatic "I-NEED-OXYGEN-with-a-THUD!!!" episode, I'm ready for just about anything from you!*

(Reflecting and grinning) Dear God,

That was SO embarrassing!

"Excuse me, nurse, but may I have a cup of 'clean' water?"

(The "Drinking" Unbeliever sips the water down, only to see a dead fly stiffly floating) "TO-TAL-L YUCK!"

(RING!!! RING!!! RING!!!)

"This water's **FIL-THY!** There's a fly in it...no, right there!! Oh-o-o-O NO! AND **two D-E-A-D gnats!!!**"

"What a **dis-as-ter!!**"

*(God looks down, leans back, drinks a cool-crisp ccup of refreshingly **CL-EEE-A-N** Frosty Ice Living Water, and chuckles while watching the "Spitting" Unbeliever's bubbly drama.)*

XXIV

∽

(Remembering the "Thud" Drama)

Dear "I NEED Spiritual OXYGEN" Unbeliever…

Yes, God?

*My Son is the **Only** One, who can work with My Spirit, to reconnect the "spirit-lifeless" back to Me.*

[Completely exasperated!] Here we go again! I'm so over Him! **Why Only** Your Son, God?

He's **way** too restrictive **for me!**

And I've just g-o-t to do **"me"**! And…

*Excuse **ME**—Dying!*

*It would be **much** better for you to "do" **My Word!***

And you say Your **Son** is **Your Word,** God?

In the Flesh!

Well—I'm sure He's a good Word, and a great Son. And since You two have a Two-layer, sorta Double connection, that's probably why You're so **partial** toward Him!

But God!

It **bothers** me that You don't <u>seem</u> to get it!

There are those who love **Y-O-U,** but just don't **choose** to do life through **Your Son!** And that's a **v-a-l-i-d** personal choice!

So-o-o, I think it would be a lot less stressful for <u>everyone</u> if You'd be just a **little** respectful of that personal-choice *b-o-u-n-d-a-r-y!*

Honestly! God—have you ever considered relaxing Your position about Your Son to fit into a slightly different perspective?!!

It's not like He's that **BIG** of a deal!

My position! My perspective! Please! So, can You respect it?

[Instrumental music with a rhythmic beat starts playing quietly in the background. The Dying Unbeliever nods "cooly" to the beat.]

[*God opens*]

Oh, I do respect it

When My Son is rejected—

*BUT that keeps **you and Me***

FULLY disconnected!

*Elimination of My **Son***

*Is the plan of My **foe…***

(DU)

But ain't love fah **only** You—

Still love—fah sho?

Dying Unbeliever!

*Watch that **slang!***

Yes—God,

It's offensive, so I shall refrain!

WOW—God! Did You hear me?

I'm bustin' BIG rhymes!

127

Yes, Rhyming Unbeliever,

But there's so LITTLE time—

And by the way!

*What's your problem with **My Son**?*

[**Music stops abruptly**]

But, why—God!???????

IS He the <u>O-N-L-Y</u> One?

Un-assured Unbeliever,

***He** gives Blessed Assurance to "reckless drivers"*

And**—you're headed toward DEATH on the freeway of **LIFE!

Oh! Dear God!

That sounds SO **not nice!**

Then—Reckless Unbeliever,

Check your brakes!

Eternity is just around death's dangerous curve!

And—you're about to have an ETERNAL COLLISION!!!

Unbeliever—I assure you, you don't want the "Eternal Boom"!

SCRE-E-E-ECH! OUCH!

Dear God!!!

I need a break!

*(Nurse! Another cup of water, please…only this time, can you substitute the floating fly for a lotta crushed ice? And a box of tissue. 'Cuz I'm **sweating** over here.)*

XXV

Dear Breaking Unbeliever,

That's a great segue into our next conversation.

On My break, I rested on the seventh day, after finalizing the Creation. I provided a beautiful place for Adam and Eve to live, and now we're going to stroll through the Garden of Eden, their first home.

How exciting, God! Are we gonna see mama* and papa?

Nope! They're not there anymore. They now live in My Forever Family Garden. We're taking this stroll because it's important that I clarify that although Adam disobeyed Me, and Adam and Eve fell into a problem, their love and deep affection for Me continued after the fall.

Well, that's good to know. But how could you tell, God?

Good question—Dying,

Despite Adam's error, he and Eve would maintain "restored connection" with Me through "willful" worship and sacrifice.

After Adam's transgression, I sent to Adam and Eve for their acceptance or rejection—what represented their second chance—the coming of My Son. They "willingly" accepted.

What did they accept—God?

Animal skins that symbolized the sacrifice they would offer to Me going forward for the atoning covering of their sins*. For an animal slain, sheds blood. And it is only by the shedding of blood that Adam's sin would be removed.

Dear God,

In English, I think that would be called "foreshadowing the plot"—a sneak preview of coming events!

That's it, "Studious" Unbeliever! The animal skins foreshadowed the coming of My Son. You didn't learn about "atonement" in your school, but it ties in. Atonement is the amends or reparation made for an injury or wrong. It's humanity's reconciliation back to Me by means of repentance and confession of one's transgressions. My Son would shed His atoning blood for humanity's restoration, for Adam's deed caused deep offense to Me—Deeply Offending Unbeliever.

Adam and Eve knew something had gone wrong, and attempted to cover themselves with a fig-leaf covering.* But their "sewing-up" a man-made solution to a spiritual problem was unacceptable to Me.

So Adam and Eve showed their willingness to accept "sin's forgiveness," on Heaven's terms—of grace, and not of human works.

132

*When they removed their "good-works" fig-leaves, and covered themselves with My "to be given" Sacrificial Provision to be slain—they made the first new-life changes through return back to Me! Adam and Eve changed from being **only** My first creation among humanity—to **becoming** My **first** son and daughter, born into My Forever Family, through acceptance of the "Coming" Second Adam—who has now Come! For without the shedding of blood, there is no remission of sin.* **

It would be the Sacrificial Lamb of God, not the-fig leaf covering of "human-works" that would solve humanity's deep spiritual problem.

See—Still Separated Unbeliever,

*The **problem with the "fig-leaf-option"** is that the fig leaves— like Adam and Eve—started dying the moment they <u>separated from their life source</u>. So **"the dying fig-leaf—intended to cover—the already "spiritually-dead" Adam and Eve,** wouldn't cut it!*

"Wilted-leaf" mama and papa. Oh—MY!

*Unto Adam also and to his wife did the LORD God make coats of skins, and clothed them. Genesis 3:21

*Endnotes

XXVI

Dear God,

Why would papa and mama even **want** to return to a fig tree—ANY kind of "fruit tree" for that matter—to get **any kind of leaves?** Because wouldn't fig leaves somehow relate to "bad-fruit" papa's **"fruit-tree" rebellion** that landed him into so much trouble in the first place?

Quite frankly, if I was papa—by now, I'da already had enough of the **"dyen' fruit tree" business! Death—death— and more death!**

Somebody should'a told papa to wake up and smell the orange juice!!!

Wake Up and Smell the Orange Juice??? What?

"Mixed-up Metaphor" Maker! Thinnnnk before you type! The expression is—"Wake up and **smell the coffee!"** *You make some* **great** *points, but T-R-Y-Y to be more mindful of your off-colored expressions!!!*

*And, as an fyi—there would be even **more** death coming down the pike. Parental Influence is **a** guaranteed reality, and the "dying-fruit" fascination caught on!*

Your distant Uncle Cain, Adam's and Eve's son, tried to bring a "dying-fruit" offering to Me that I rejected—there was no "life"—no blood in it! So sadly, he found out the hard way that when it comes "spiritual" business, humanity MUST conduct this business RIGHT.

Dear God,

What is right?

*"Right" is whatever is done according to My specified guidelines. "Right" connects to My "righteousness" and leads to life in Me. Many do not realize it, but it's humanity's prideful rebellion that leads to **"bloodless-lifeless** spiritual worship" that I must reject, just as I did Cain's.*

You see—any "substitute" that attempts to replace My Son—and connect to Me through another god(s) or human-works—is fruit that will wilt in eternity. Such "lifeless fruit" is unable to produce eternal life in Me—since disconnected from My Son.

"Substituting" Unbeliever,

It's a "dead-fly" in the Water of Life, and I cannot accept it—as there is Only ONE life-giving God!

Oh—My—God!

I'm starting to see where Your Son gets His narrow **"exclusivity—only ONE"** thinking! You Two sound just a-like! He says, there's Only ONE Way to "the Father," and that's through Him. And You say, You're the **Only ONE God— and You're His Father!** So, I guess You'd both say—the only "right" way to You—as His Father, is through Your Son's "ONE" blood?

Yep. For it is out of "HIS" blood My Spiritual Nation will be born.

Dear "All-Inclusive" Unbeliever.

Here's the deal!

Anyone who claims "acceptance" of My Son

but denies the need for His cleansing, life-giving blood

OR any who replace the acceptance of My Son with human works efforts to "do" "My Will—," as God "pleasers"

***OR tries to** "neatly" fit My Son in*

with a list of "other" gods

as a "one-among-many" option for humanity...

...is wearing a "withering" fig-leaf God?

*Yep. The deceiver owns the attractive and popular **"Withering- Leaves" by the Lie-Giver** fashion line!*

His "temporary-life wear" looks good on earth, but unravels at the seams in eternity.

So Withering "Fig-Leaf" Fashion Wearer!

You're just not matching with My Word!

(Ring…Ring) Excuse me nurse, but may I see a mirror? I thought my life was matching! Thank you.

XXVII

⌒⌒⌒

Dear God,

What rhymes with "eternity?"

Paternity—why?

Because I might have a good one! "Fig-leaves" wither in Eternity!!! 'Cuz they can't shed blood for paternity. (hilarious laughing that abruptly stops.)

[Awkward silence]

…so, You don't think that's f-unn-y, God?

Nope.

A dud? Sorry, God! I think You're ready to move on…

Yep.

XXVIII

[Quickly moving on] ...so God, animal sacrifice to cover papa's filth and stain was a pretty big deal to You. Right?

It was.

But why involve innocent animals, God?

Because, unlike Adam, animals had never become defiled by sin. Therefore, the blood of animals remained pure, and could thus "cover" humanity's sin temporarily. Until the coming of My Perfect Lamb, assigned to the "permanent sin-removal" task, clean animals would do.

But God? Why "double-trouble?"

Since You used animal skins, wouldn't that mean precious animals would've had to die? **And** "Your Lamb" had to be slain, **too?** Total OUCH! Wasn't all this animal slaying just a tad bit of "overkill?" Because, if animals were **already** being slain, then why did **"Your Son"** have to die, too?

Perplexed Unbeliever—Great Question!

While the blood of animals was pure (since none in My animal kingdom had ever sinned, and thus had not fallen) still, the animal experience was limited in its effectiveness to address Adam's plight.

Limited? How God? Why?

*Well, Adam needed Someone who could offer a two-layered solution. Not only did he need a pure sacrifice to be made on his behalf (this would call for the purity of an animal.) But Adam also needed Someone to Sacrifice who could enter into his sinful experience (this would call for a Pure Man who could face the God/god temptation and **also** choose.)*

*Adam was guilty—at-fault as the **man** who created humanity's "death and debt" problem. So according to the legalities of My Divine Justice, it had to be a **Man** who would fix it! Thus, there was the need for animals to "temporarily" cover Adam's sin, and the Human Lamb of God to remove it.*

So, until His coming to permanently remove humanity's stain of sin, the pure blood of pure animals slain, would do.

Innocent animal slayin'? Dear God!

YUCKITY! Yucks! **And more yucks!** As the Creator of even animals, didn't You have had a problem with Your **innocent** animals being killed?

Dear Rightfully Concerned,

I made animals for many reasons, and care about them, too. But just as any father would do if faced with the choice between the death of his animal, or the death of his child; the child would win out every time. Thus—I, as the Loving Heavenly Father, chose. The slaying of animals insured that My Forever Family members could die in the faith, covered by the shed blood of "atoning" animals, until the coming of My Son...

Lost Unbeliever,

I sent My Lamb down to help the lost of the earth find their way "Home,"* for ALL who will follow.

Awwwe. God. That's sweet!

It reminds me of, "Mary had a little lamb

143

Its fleece was white as snow

And every where that Mary went

The lamb was sure to go"!

"Nursery Rhyming" Unbeliever,

As the Loving Father, who wanted to keep connection with those who loved Me before the coming of My Son, I assigned humanity's High Priests to enter into the Holy of Holies once a year on the Day of Atonement. They would present the blood of animals, as the sacrificial offering.

So, because of the blood, I was able keep relationship with My People until the coming of My Son. The horrible disgust of the sins of the people was covered. And I saw not the filthy stain of Adam's sin, but the loving hearts of sacrifice and worship made unto Me. All parties were pleased. I was satisfied. And My people went away "covered by the blood" and relieved to have effectively dealt with the burden of their unrighteousness.

"Animal-Loving"—Unbeliever,

It was out of concern for humanity's connection back to Me that I enlisted, first the unstained "hoofs," and then the Unstained "Nail-Scarred Hands" to help deal with Adam's sin.

Born in a manger with lowly animals, My Son was humanity's Sacrificial Lamb. And presenting His atoning blood to Me, on behalf of the people, He was humanity's High Priest. While on the Cross He entered into the Holy of Holies Once and for All,** and presented Himself as the Unblemished Offering unto to Me.

He Finished His Work! Now, there is **no** *further need for "little lambs" to be slain for humanity's transgressions. In My Son's Words, "It is Finished!"*

But,

God. Just knowing that You allowed precious, innocent little lambs to help my papa's mess is SUPERLY disgusting to me!

Dear "SUPERLY" Not Innocent Unbeliever,

What would you do if there were dead bodies in your house that were uncovered and attracting flies?

And because of the "death-contaminated" conditions

unless something was done

all of your friends would need to stay away from you

because time was needed

before **Someone** *could*

arrive to remove them,

along with their offensive odor?

YUCKY, YUCKY, and **yucky** again God!

I would **cover** them!

Dying Unbeliever,

*That's **exactly** what I did!*

with the blood of earth's innocent lambs

until Heaven's Innocent Lamb would arrive!!!

*Endnotes

XXX

Dear God,

I now know from You that Adam is my original dad.

But I was taught that "Chimp-Chimp,"

Rover and Fido are ALSO my distant kin.

God, are they r-e-ally-y My siblings???

They're *so-o* cute!

"Barking" Unbeliever???

Rover? Fido—? as in "roof, roof"?

Yes, God.

And "Chimp-Chimp," the Chimpanzee!

They're **absolutely** a-dor-a-ble!

Are they a **connected** part of the family???

…so smart—caring and *cute, cute, cute!*

*"Evolved, **'Animal-Connected'"** Unbeliever,*

Let me share with you the Pecking Order

of Creation

and where I, with thought, placed the animals.

Let's start with the angels

I created the angels significantly lower than Myself

I made Adam a little lower than the angels*

And the animals a lot lower than Adam

For I did not place eternityin the hearts of earth's animals, *

but I placed it in the hearts of humanity.

Adam's animals would provide assistance

and enjoyment for him...

...as My People on the earth—provide for Me.

*I did not give animals free will to choose between God or evil...
nor, did I give them dominion to rule over My earth. **

This dominion, I gave to humanity—through Adam!

So, when Old Serpent showed up in the Garden to attack My **Spoken** Word—He **spoke** deception, not to an animal, but to Eve who could ALSO **speak** about God—and discern—!*

*I **spoke** to Adam*

The Word of My Law

as I created Adam

In My image

and in My likeness

for I ALSO Reason and CHOOSE

as does Satan

who chose against Me!

*That deceiver could **not** have convinced an animal to oppose My Word!*

For while I deposited vast,

"earthly" reasoning capacity into animals

they do not make eternal decisions of the heart.

*Endnotes

*He has made everything beautiful in its time. He has also set eternity in the hearts of men (Ecclesiastes 3:11).

XXXI

I breathed My breath of life into Adam and connected him to the Life of My Spirit. And I gave life's breath, also to animals. But when I breathed My breath into Adam, he became a living soul*—with a will, to choose between either God or god?

When I connected Adam's human spirit to My life-giving Spirit—he became a living spirit, with a power-for-life connection to Me.

But, when "connected" Adam, polluted with death My "life-giving" deposit of blood, which spilled into ALL humanity—the Second Adam came. With Unstained Blood to purify all who will receive Him—, he offers humanity reconnection back to Me, as My cleansing Word.

*And the LORD God formed man of the dust of the ground, and breathed into his nostrils the breath of life; and man became a living soul. Genesis 2:7

XXXII

Word! Word! Word! Blood! Blood! **Blood!** And More Blood!!
Okay. But God,

You're making a **plenty big deal** about your Son's blood,
but what about this? What about the boundaries of time
and direction? What about those who were **not** alive on the
earth **before and after** His "bleeding sacrifice" was made?
Wouldn't that make Your Son's blood of no effect to them?

Wouldn't His "purifying work" have **missed** ALL those who
needed "cleansing," but **preceded and followed** His coming down here? For example, those who went as far back as
Adam and Eve, and the others who died before Your Son
came—wouldn't His "cleansing" blood have missed them
completely? Earth's history would agree that there's a great
time lapse between the time of the ancient "stained ones" of
old, and the time of the shedding of Your Son's blood on the
earth. With a "gap-in-time" problem, wouldn't that compromise the effectiveness of Your Son's work? Truthfully God,
maybe the "Power of the Blood" has limits!

XXXIII

NO *"Limiting" Unbeliever!!!*

There is NO limit to the Dynamic Penetrating Power of My Son's Infinite blood! Because there's no limit His Infinite Power in Me.

My Son's blood IS ETERNALLY ALIVE—Because it's drawn from My Fountain of "Eternal" Life!

It's EVERLASTING with "FOREVERMORE" Wonder-Working Power results!!!

*His Precious Blood is **always** Flowing!*

*It's **always** Powerful!*

*It's **always** Available!*

*And it's **Eternally Capable!***

***Not** bound by the limits of time or direction on earth!*

***Not** limited by the boundaries of the—past, present, or future!*

Since transported by My "Moving" Spirit!

Which was poured out on the earth after My Son returned Home

To indwell the "blood-washed" with LIVING POWER!

*His Blood pours for **EVERMORE!***

It flows in all directions—both forward AND backward—always working—NEVER to STOP!

(Having fun) But, what about backwards, God?

Yes! It's retroactive to cover ALL those who died in the faith—covered temporarily by the blood of the animals slain—even as far back as Abraham, Moses, and Adam and Eve.

(Enjoying the unlimited directions) And can that blood "flow in forward"—like a fast car, God?

Yep! The cleansing blood flows forward today—cleansing <u>ALL</u> who will receive Him both now, and in the future! And as the Father, I love it! Because accepting the Blood of My Son—which flows through the Power of My Spirit—initiates the "new-births" of My "cleansed, new-life babies." And each "receiving will" is a "ready womb."

Dear God,

Can it run—EVEN SIDE **W-A-Z-E!** [Smiles]

*Okay, **Silly One!** Yep. It can run even "Side-W-a-z-e"! [Smiles returned...]*

ZIG-ZAG?

Yep. Now, back to work!

Work! Work—Chicken *(baawk)* burk! (giggling) Okay, God.

XXXIV

Dear God,

New births are really important to You, aren't they?

Dear "Not-Yet Birthed" Unbeliever,

As the Only Eternal Father, I've always wanted a BIG Family. So I keep busy drawing hearts and wills to My Son—through the Power of My Spirit. For none can come to My Son unless I draw them. *

"Up" to You, God? (Imagining) Then You have a "Forever Family Ladder"—for "climbing up" up to You, right, God?

*No one can come to Me, except My Father who sent Me draw them (John 6:44).

XXXV

Dear "Imagining" Unbeliever,

Imagine this...there are fountains of water in the earth's terrain, but not fountains of blood.

I can "see" that, God. But why are there no fountains of blood on earth?

Because "Earthly" Unbeliever,

*Blood is not an "earthly," but a Heavenly resource. Consequently, although it flows through human veins, it has a spiritual connection. When cleansed—"cleansed blood" supports "separated life" back to new life in Me, since no longer stained with death. In Heaven, blood is highly protected as My biological "life-**giving**" agent, as passed on by First Adam. It is My "life-**cleansing**" agent that was shed by Second Adam for humanity's reconnection. So, not only does it help sustain the biological life of the flesh, but it also helps Me identify who has accepted or rejected the "cleansing-life" of My Son. That is its spiritual life or death function. When My Son does **not** sign off on a "cleansed-life," I do not issue that individual a "new-birth" connection back to* *life in Me. You see—that's why My Son insists, "None comes to the Father, but by Me."*

(Excitedly) So, God, what is my spritiual blood type?

*Well **"Type D"** Unbeliev...*

(Interrupts excitedly) I have Type-D blood, God? What does the "D" stand for?!!

*"**D**eath—through fallen Adam."*

(Much less excited.) Oh. Can we just **move** on?

Yep. New topic! Let's leave "blood groups" and head to "blood groupings."

There are TWO spiritual blood type groups. The blood-type grouping that connects you to the fallen father, through first Adam—or the Reigning Father, through Risen Second Adam, the Son!

You see, Dying Unbeleiver,

There is a fountain filled with blood, drawn from Emmanuel's veins, and sinners plunged beneath that flood lose all their guilty stains!

(Completely exasperated—AGAIN.) But God!

There **h-a-s** to be MORE to Your Son than JUST Blood, Blood, **Blood!** Does it NEVER run out? When does it stop??

Dying Unbeliever!

*It never stops! It reaches to the highest mountain and flows to the lowest valley! His blood that gives great strength from **day-to-day** will NEVER lose its Power!**

Well, God. I guess!

Concept taken from Lyrics from "The Blood Will Never Lose Its Power" by Andre Crouch (1969).

XXXVI

Guessing Unbeliever,

*But when will you choose **to know?***

To believe?

To receive?

*To have receiving **FAITH** to accept My Son?*

Sorry, God,

Sorry! I TOTALLY apologize but there's **a lot of other ways** for people to express their faith! Like me, for example I have **faith** in my ability to help make the planet a better place!

Making the earth a better place definitely has its place!

Improver of the Planet,

But, priorities of the earth that lose focus on the need for recon-nection with Me will ultimately pose a problem for a desireable eternity.

Eternity!

Eternity!

Eternity!

But what about the **here and now,** God? There's nothing wrong with a few good deeds to help improve life down here—TODAY!

Dear "Here Today and Gone Tomorrow" Unbeliever!

*Time so q-u-i-c-k-l-y passes! The good works that some complete—even acts of **exceptionally good deeds**—without the acceptance of My Son...*

Dear God!

Dead deal?

Yep!

Dead deal!

What about major contributions, God?

Even major contributions to good causes, such as donations to effective ministries—that's good—but without My Son...

Still. Dead deal?

No deal!

Really, God?

Even the **HEFTY** donation I gave when I got my settlement from that grocery cart accident! Getting' hit during the peak rush hour over there at the Super Store got me well over $30.00! You remember that one, God? **Hit and run...** Unreal!

Yep, "Big" Contributor—with Whip Lash!!!

I remember. But—No deal.

Any effort made on the part of humanity toward earning "God points," but is separate from My Son adds up to no deal!

And all attempts to connect with Me, but exclude the Work of My Son is as of filthy rags in my sight.

Wait—dead and Filthy?

Really, God?

Not useable at **all?**

Nope.

Not if humanity attempts to come to Me by a stack of dead human works that bypass My Son!

Honestly God,

I think that's why so many **don't** take YOUR SON *as* a deal! Because it's really too much!

Just *His* Work, and none of ours? I would think what humanity brings to the table should have *some* merit!—even i-f it IS dead!!!

Dead "Merit and Works" Unbeliever,

*Humanity's deeds do good on many fronts, but they **cannot** be exchanged for eternal life!*

It's only those who are cleansed by the Blood of the Lamb,

*overcome by the word of their acceptance of **Him**—*

and who make a changed-life commitment,

who can come to reside with Me!

See God,

Too demanding!

Just **too** demanding! Wantin' people to change their words and lives—**while You** discount their "good" works as just dead junk is just W-A-Y over the top!

And folks having to give up their OWN way to start in Your Son's direction is…well, downright unreasonable! And to be honest, I feel it's a shaky assumption that folks even **want** to change!

Dear God,

I would think that by now you would know that down here—for the most part, we do life OUR own way!

Or, at least that's how I do mine. And personally—at this point, I'm sure it would be kinda too late for me to leave my *own* path to follow **Your Son's directions!! So, I don't even plan to try.**

Well, Now, Listen Here! "Soon to be Traveling" Unbeliever!

*You will be trying to get to **"His"** Father's **House** won't you?*

His **What? Who?**

"My Son's Father's" House!—

OH! Yes, God! I'm trying to get there.

*Then follow **HIS** directions!*

But God, ex-act-ly! **I'M** trying to get to Your "Son's *FATHER'S"* House!

So, when did *HE* start runnin' the Place—like it's **HIS?**

Likely, He'll be expecting me to have made a **"full-life"** com-mitment to **H-I-M!** And that just happens **not** to be MY plan! (Thinks without typing to try to insure that God won't hear.) He is SO Self-Centered!

Come on, God. Let's just be real—doing things Your Son's WAY would take an act of God!!

XXXVII

"Self-Centered" Unbeliever,

Exactly!

And that's why you need the Power of My Spirit to change! U-Turning from death to eternal life is a GREAT DIRECTION—change!!!

XXXVIII

Hold Up, God!

I hear You! But I'm **ALSO** startin' to see a pattern. You keep wanting me to **believe** that Your Son turned a lot of this "certain-death" stuff around!

You say He has "U-Turnin' life-changin'" Power, but from the way I see it! **Everybody** ends up dead!

Papa died! Animals died! And even though Your Son might've turned things around for HIMSELF, **EVEN He died, too! And now it's <u>my</u> turn!**

"Good" Lord???

So, I'm wondering if this optimistic **"death-to-eternal-life"** picture is not quite as glamorous as You're trying to **paint it** to be. Just sayin'!

And in ALL due respect to Your **"life outta death"** viewpoint, God—but I'd like get this off my chest once and for ALL! Here's what **I've** noticed. This human **race** is a pretty tough one! "On your mark. Get set. Die! Everybody starts out liven', stumbles up on some pain, and then ends up 6 feet under—graveyard DEAD!!! Kaput! Deuces!

So, Honestly God!

"Forbidden Fruit" Papa r-e-a-l-l-y **blew it!** He blew it for **EVERYONE who landed on earth,** and right about now, I'm starting to wonder if <u>You</u> even care? Cuz, if you did— why don't you **stop the trouble?**

And not to be <u>rude</u>, but even though You say Your Son came down to make things better, (and **fortunate for Him, He got out alive**—) Your world is still a tough one! JUST keep breathing, and death'll pop up **somewhere** and **nail** you after a while! But, unlike Your Son—I'm still not sure WHO'S gonna get me up???

And one last thing! If Your Son's <u>really</u> **all about LIFE,** then where is He when somebody's dying, and needs **a lift?**

And for that matter, God.

[The Dying Unbeliever takes a fork and a knife and creates a make-shift set of drum sticks. "Playing the drums" on the hospital food cart, while singing self-pitily in A flat—**very flat, the "singer of the blues" blurts out.**]

[Woefully humming] Soon I will be done with the troubah of dis world! The troubah of dis world! **YOU-WHOOO** The trou-bah of dis (fades)... Troubl's on me like a cactus, and I might not see **dayeeeee!** Death's on me like back taxes, and I gotstah **payeee! Gottsta payee**—Might not see **day-eeeeeeeee...**'Cuzz ain't no sunshine when it's goooonne...

(Interrupts) F-l-l-a-t Hummen' 'n DRUMMEN' Unbeliever!!!!!! STOPIT!

XXXIX

[stunned] Yes—God?

*Are you **finished?***

Well—I guess!

*Well—I **hope** so!*

"God-Blaming" Critic!

*Because **I gave dominion of the world to Adam—the head of** YOUR family—the condition the world is in is <u>N-O-T</u> of **My** doing. Adam left M-Y path, and humanity walked in **its own way**—into its **own destruction!** Adam rebelled. And for a specific reason, I put Adam and Eve out of the comfortable home I built for them.* Their loss of the Paradise I prepared for their provision, protection, and pleasure hurt me deeply. Adam cursed the ground from which he was created because of **his** willful dis-obedience.* Thus, **Adam and Eve walked out of the Garden of Eden into the hostile world in which humanity lives today!*** So what you blame ME for are just the sorrowful results of Adam's rebelling direction as humanity's universal father.*

(Awkward pause)

[Just a quiet whisper. *(sorry God)* The "Ranting" Unbeliever feels clearly embarrassed after getting "spanked" for "the rant" that upset God.]

most dearest

nicet'st God

You are so nice

are You still speaking to

Me?

type yes or no

Dying Unbeliever,

Barely! *But I'm still speaking. So, let Me finish.*

[Louder whisper.] Okay, God. (Thinks to self—"Oh, Thank God" He hasn't given up on me! [Quickly picking up confidence.]

Then let's keep movin', God!

Yep—Let's! Now, here's what I want you to know. As humanity's Creator, I've done My part to make things better. I gave My Son—My Son gave His life, so that might eat from the Tree of Life—in My Garden. The Invitation has been sent out to "Come *and dine"! **And** My Son is preparing a Brand New Home* for OUR New Family. And it's **much** better than what I built down there for Adam and Eve.*

Yes! *Things can get discouragingly dark in the earth; but He IS the Light of the World, the Restorer of life, and He offers rest for the weary!*

Weary Unbeliever...

[Wearily] Yes, God?

As the One who tasted humanity's death, My Son IS the Compassionate Entrance into My Eternal Home. For the present and the future—He offers peace, joy, and power for Living to those who trust in Him.

"God-surrender" does not make life ALL perfect, but it makes it ALL worth while—and possible!

Restless Unbeliver,

*With burdens and cares...how 'bout you come to Him. He **will** give you rest!* For My Son does My Will. And as the Father, **My Will** is that weary humanity enter into His rest, and thus rest— **In Me.** For there is a rest for the People of God.**

[Quiet]

*"There remaineth therefore a rest to the people of God." Hebrews 4:9

*Endnotes

XL

Caring God,

Thanks. Yes, I am tired, and really scared. I know it **probably** looks like You're not getting through to me, but I've been kinda reflecting on Your words.

Dear God,

Lots of **my words** are spoken from defense and pain.

I imagine that's the case with a lot of people. Truthfully, I've been wondering, when You look at hurting humanity, **exactly** what do You see?

Dear Dyi-ver,

[Interrupting] Dear—**Dyi-ver?**

God,

Did You just give me a **nickname?**

Yep! Afterall, you called Me "Caring!" Do you like it?

(Repeating God's word from the last email.) "Barely!" But, I'll accept it since it's coming from You. (chuckles)

[Chuckles] *Good.*

Was it easy for you to come up with it, God?

Quite. I reduced "Dyi"ng to "Dyi," and I took the "ver" off of Unbelie"ver" to create "Dyi-ver."

Dear God,

To be honest, I LOVE my new nickname! It's nice.

Then it's "gonna stick"! Let's carry on! While people look at the outward appearance, I see deeper. I see the hurting heart.

Oh God!

How deeply do You see humanity's pain? How deeply do you see the hurt **I feel?**

Dear "Becoming More Real—"

*I see the **real**, underlying condition of each hurting life!*

I see beyond the masks that are worn and the anger released, and I see the unmasked condition of each wounded soul!

[Feeling a little "too" affectionate] Dear God,

May I call You "**Heavy G**"?

Dear Dyi-ver,

*Do you understand a **Healthy** NO?*

(Grinning) Sorry, kind Sir!

Okay—Courteous Dyi-ver,

Now, where were we?

Dear Sir! My heart has ached a lot in my life time!

Dying Unbeliever,

Life can be a heart-acher and a will-breaker!

That's why finding relationship with Me is so important. I long for those who have not yet said, "Father, by entrance through Your Son—I need you!"

God,

Have You EVER considered that "father" can sometimes be *such* a hurting word?

XLI

"Heavenly Fatherless" Unbeliever,

I understand. But despite that many among humanity have been disappointed by a father—fatherhood is still a role of great importance in a life.

So, I mercifully wait for each who will choose to become MY child!

I see, Heavenly Fath... Oops, I Mean...[feeling conflicted] G-od.

Then, as a Father, do You see the hearts of those who are sad...not understanding why You won't fix their b-r-o-k-e-n situation?

Dyi-ver, I do!

Well then—God,

Why won't you fix mine? Why won't you stop **my** pain?

Deeply Broken One,

Often, I'm blamed for the work of the wicked one who has come, **broken,** *killed, and destroyed. Also, I'm regularly held responsible for the brokeness so many have brought upon themselves.*

Notwithstanding, I know that the greatest miracle for any hopeless situation is the restoring of one's soul, and the returning to life in Me, through My Son. So, sometimes I use pain as the **only** *tool that allows My Word to penetrate the "hurting" place when one, otherwise, might roam too far.*

It's in timing. It's in **willful turning** *that healing happens. Unbeliever, that's when a wanderer becomes My child!*

God—

Am I your child?

Wandering and Wondering Unbeliever,

Not yet!

My creation includes ALL My handiwork. But the Father/child relationship is reserved exclusively for those who establish Parent/ child relationship with Me—through My—

—Son!

God, I'm starting to understand Your perspective...how You think!

And—God,

I imagine You're a Great Dad?

Beloved, Dyi-ver...

I Am!

*And when you become My child—you won't have to ask. You'll no longer wonder...you will **know**!*

Wow—You sound like a re-a-lly *Great Dad!* So what do Your children say about Your parenting style?

My ma-ture children say I allow them deep pain to learn to trust My caring Hands. But then I hold them close, through My Son's nail-scarred Hands, and there—in closeness—We heal their wounds—while watching them grow up in My Word!

But God, that sounds like such a contradiction. How can You be a good Parent, **but** still allow deep pain in the life of Your children?

Insightful Unbeliever—That's why My immature children always complain!

But—Dying Unbeliever,

*For **full** insight, you'd have to speak to **My Son!** As My Word made flesh, He died on the Cross. He suffered, bled, and died— sacrificially! But it was **deep** pain with **deep** purpose!*

Dying Unbeliever, the deep pain I allow in the lives of My children always has deep purpose!

De-e-e-p purpose in *de-e-e-p* pain?

<u>*What*</u> God?

I never heard of such! That concept must be ***b-r-rand*** new!

XLII

Dyi-ver,

*There's nothing **new** under the sun.* *

Really? God,

Then if nothing's new—what do You consider the *ole'* stuff?

"Ole' stuff?"

Dyi-ver, are you back to using that slang?

Oh, No Sir, God.

That's just "modern."

*"Modern?" Oh. Well, here's one example of something **old:** When Adam fell, the tempter wanted Me to abandon ALL humanity!*

So, God,

What's **"<u>old</u>"** about that?

Dyi-ver,

*Satan was hoping that I'd sit just sit back and take his **punch.** He wanted Me to leave Adam and **A-L-L** of Adam' family under the power of his "death-grip," eternally—**But over 2,000 years ago,** MY Son accepted the "DG Reverse" Challenge, and then He got involved in the SDB!*

Over 2,000 years? Now that's OLD! But, what kinda "Reverse," God?

Oh, that would be the Death-Grip Reverse!

Got it! And the **SDB?** What's that?

*That's the Spirituall **Death** Business!*

And, I must say, Dyi-ver! My Son handled HIS Business! (Personal Note: Oh, My—When it comes to talkin' about My Son's Victory, I'm startin' to sound kinda like Dyi-ver. What He did to Satan gets me talkin' kinda fast!)

So, Your Son turned things around? How, God?

Yep. My Word got Personally involved,

*And Dyi, He turned death in **Our** favor!*

Death got turned around in Y-O-U-R favor, God? Kinda like a "turn-around" in a football game when the team that looked like it was getting' spanked makes a come back!!

Yep. That's what I'm talking about! Just when it looked like My enemy's team was winning with Adam's "first-down/fully-down" defeat, My Son came to earth's field and made a "tomb-emptying" play.

(God-animated) DYI-VER,

*He turned the "death" play around so that death started working for ME! Now—ANY spiritually **"dead"** person who receives MY SON—becomes **dead** to the **death of sin!** So, the dead in Adam—who started out spiritually **"dead"** are NO longer **"dead in sin"** but **alive** in **MY SON'S** righteousness, AND made **"brand new"** in ME!*

Wow, God!

Sounds like You know a li'l some'um about **football!!!**

*So there is nothing new under the sun. Ecclesiastes 1:9

Endnotes

XLIII

Sports Dyi-ver!

Try Me!

Okay—Captain!

Let's talk about an interception—(something I'm not sure You'd know about)—changes the direction of a play!

So, here's my first question: In a professional football game, what do You call this? The quarterback, in an attempt to make a touchdown, throws the football to his team member, but a player from the opposing team catches the ball and runs it toward **his** team's touchdown zone—and scores?

"Touchdown" Dyi-ver!

That is an...

...let me help You, God!

It's an IN-TER-CEP-TION.

The intercepting team has **reversed** the direction of the play!

Next question, God. Ready?

Yep!

Good. Now, this one might be a little hard for You, God. When the intercepting team makes a touchdown, the scoring team gets added points on the scoreboard that reflect what happened.

The ball is now moving in a reversed direction—toward a "touchdown" of "unexpected" victory! The runner is A-L-L out front blowin' dust in the opposer's face, an...

...Just like My Son, Dyi-ver! That was My Son!

It WAS AN UPSET!

*The scoreboard was looking **hopeless** for ETERNAL LIFE! The opposing team had scored what looked like an irreversable victory for Eternal Death when Adam—*

Did the all-time greatest **"forbidden'-fruit" fumble** in football history?

*Which landed him straight into the Dead-End Zone of **eternal death!***

*But **My** Son*

Left Heaven

Landed on Earth's Football Field

Ran to the Cross SNATCHED Death

*And in a **REVERSE** Play*

Took Adam's Penalty

(Angels cheer) "Run Word, Run!!!"

Scored the ETERNAL

TOUCHDOWN!!!

Satan's DEFEAT!!!!!!!!

YEEAAAAAAA-Y-Y-Y-Y-Y

Angels and Dyi-ver!

*You got Me **STANDING!***

That sounds a might like PRAISE!

*That was **MY** SON running the Ball of Resurrection*

Y-E-SS! HE REVERSED THE WHOLE GAME!!!

Dear God,

I didn't know You can stand!

*Oh—I WILL arise when My enemy is **SCA-T-TERED!****

And I **re-a-l-ly** didn't know You're an avid football fan!

Well, Dyi-ver!

***Most** folks don't!*

So God, which is **Your** team during the Playoffs?

"Playoffs" Dyi-ver,

*I'm **always** on the side of the team that's winnen'! And listen to this, Lil' Sport. How 'bout I tell you about MY Franchise!*

"Football"—God?

I didn't know You own a **Football Franchise!**

Oh, Yes! Sport!

*My Son is My Team Captain **and** My Star Player! He ran head-on into My enemy, the Contaminator, and **CRUSHED** his **head!*****

Dear God,

So, no helmet?

Dyi-ver,

He didn't see it comin'!

What's his nick-name on the field?

Slew-foot! Yep. Slew-foot got...

...rolled on?

Yep. "rolled on," Dyi-ver!

Go God! You the Man!

No, Forgeting Unbeliever

You keep forgetting! My SON is the Man!

*And anybody who wants to play on **My** team has to join the wide receivers!*

Dear God,

The **wide** "whats?"

*The wide **receivers**!*

Dyi-ver,

You must **receive** *The Team Captain to be recruited onto My Team!*

Gotta team name?

Death Raiders!

Cheerleaders?

The Unstained Praisers!

Mascot?

The Resurrected Lamb!

Team colors?

Crimson "Blood" Red!

Game Schedule?

He's returning soon!

For the Final Game

Y-A-AY GOD!

Good stats?

Dyi-ver,

It was a great winning season! My Son lived without sin, died without stain, successfully completed His attempt on Calvary! And BUSTED out smooth from the enemy's choke-hold!

Busted out **cl-ean?**

*Clean as His EMPTY TOMB! He took humanity's game to a **whole** new level! Now He's the ONLY Star in the Resurrection Hall of Faith!*

And Dyi-ver!

Come to think of it, it's no wonder why He calls Himself

THE RESURRECTION!!!

Boy! That Fella is SOMETHING ELSE!

*Let God arise, let his enemies be scattered (Psalm 68:1).

**He will crush your head, and you will strike his heel" (Genesis 3:15 BSB).

**Endnotes

XLIV

WOW, God!

I must admit You tell a GREAT story. And I'm not tryin' to make Your Team <u>look</u> bad, but if Your Son's *such* a Star, why'd He go out on the Cross lookin' **straight** defeated?

Truth be told, folks say in the Cross Quarter, looks like **HE'S** the one who got spanked!

I heard even His closest following fans agree that He got **r-eal-l-l** bloodied up on Day 1!

Yep! He did.

But Day 3, Dying Unbeliever! On that Third Day, He brought the crowd up to its feet!

*I'll be the first to admit, My Son's performance at Calvary started out looking <u>real</u> bad. But here's a little inside team information—it was a **strategic** move to fulfill My Divine Justice for Adam's "off-side" penalty!*

Papa fouled out for ignoring **basic** instructions on the field, God?

Yep. "Keep the evil out of your system, and stay in the safety zone!" That's how I coached him at every practice! But Adam STILL ended up in the dead-end zone, and made an offensive foul—against Me!

Fumblin'-fouler!! God, papa really played a really **lousy** game!

He sure did, Dyi-ver!

But because he and Eve put My jersey on after Adam went off-sides—I didn't drop them from the team!

What was Your jersey, God?

Dyi-ver,

My jersey was the animal skins that symbolized the coming of My Son. Covering up with My skins expressed their willingness to be washed by the blood, and receive My pardon.

Pops and moms!! **Work it!** Strut yo' skins an' drop THAT fig leaf like it's…**h-o-t!** Pops, you **k-n-o-w** you blew it!!!

Dyi-ver!

Yes, God?

You're Done!

[Tries to suppress giggling] Yes, Sir!

XLV

[Trying to become serious, the Dying Unbeliever moves to a serious topic.]

So, God,

Making a lousy play in life doesn't <u>automatically</u> block someone from joining Your team?

Nope! But Dyi-ver, "drop that fig leaf like it's hot?" And slamming your original dad like that? You know better! When do you plan to put a filter on that mouth?

I know God, and I'm workin' on it. Sometimes papa's stain just gets the best of me. Puttin' it out there only for folks to get upset is getting' old. And I'm gettin' tired of my mouth gettin' me in **boiling hot** water!!!

Dear God,

Like those people on T.V.—I need someone to fix my life!

Reference to Oprah Winfrey Network's: Fix My Life

Dyi-ver,

One *of the hats My Son wears is that of the Master Life-RepairMan!**

*For all have sinned and come short off the glory of God. Romans 3:23

XLVI

(Corny joke) So, God—Your Son wears only ONE hat, but I wear **two!**

[Excited] That's it! TWO HATS!

Dear Dyi-ver,

Two Hats.

Two Hats? Come again, God? I was just playin'!

I know—but this will REALLY help you see It!

See what, God?

That My Son wears two hats!

Two hats. That's totally cool!

But wait a minute! Two hats? What does that have to *do* with *anything?*

Oh, Dyi-ver, it has to do with <u>everything</u>!

The first hat=God, and the other hat=Man (humanity.)

Oh, Okay? And then what?

Dying Unbeliever,

Hat 1:

*He's God—**My Eternal Word.***

Hat 2:

I wrapped My Eternal Word

in Human Flesh—a Body

to become My Son

the Earth's Second Adam

to join humanity

*as Earth's Redeeming **Man!!!***

Okay God, So?

So there are two sides!

XLVII

Huh…Two sides of what, God?

Dyi-ver,

There are two sides of My Son's family!

His mother's side, and My side, as His Father!

Okay, God!

Now that's super basic, cuz there's also two sides to mine—
my mother's side and my father's side!

So, what's the point?

Dyi-ver, in My Son's case, it's much more complicated!

God, re-a-lly.

Why does just about **everything** about Your Son have to be
so comm-pli-ca-ted??!

Dear Comm-pli-ca-ted Unbeliever!

Putting My Eternal Word into an Earthen Body had its own complications! Plus, He entered into a complicated situation.

And, JUST as My experience has been COMPLICATED working with **you**—*working to save humanity IS A VERY* **complicated** *undertaking!*

Wel-l, **"OU-CH"!**

(~Confidential Note~)

(Dear God, Am I <u>re-al-ly</u> hard to work with? Please don't show this to anyone—not even Your Son!)

(Dear Dyi-ver, you are both fun to work with, and also **a bit** *of a challenge! Since I'm God—I'm up to it, but you're definitely giving Me a full-Spirit workout!)*

(Duly noted! And <u>ple-ase</u> put my note in Your shredder!)

"Hiding" Unbeliever! My Son **IS** *the Shredder.*

Well…that's **just** GREAT! And **n-o-w** You tell me!

Dear God,

So why is Your Son **A-L-L-L** in Your Business?!

NOSEY UNBELIEVER! CHECK YOURSELF AND STAY IN YO-UR LANE!!!!

*My Son **Transacts** My Business! My Son Is **My Word!!!***

***Real-ly-y** Dyi-ver!*

*I don't like it when I go there, but when you talk about **MY SON**, you talkin' about ME—AND you gonna get set straight!!!*

*And while I'm at it—**just Who** do you think created the Universe?* A-n-d sustains it now—**and** turned on the Lights!!!** MY WORD! And don't you type anything right now—you just learn some'um, Mouthy Unbeliever!!!*

*Endnotes

XLVIII

(Blank stare)

So, where was I? Oh, that's right, I was talking about family "sides." My Son's Father's side connects Him to heaven, and His mother's side connects Him to earth!

Got it, God! You haven't lost me yet! And believe me. I'm gonna stay offa **T-H-A-T** nerve.

*(Without missing a beat—) Good. And His **DUAL** nature was necessary for Him to carry out His divine assignment, as humanity's Redeeming Deliverer.*

(Extra respectfully) Dear God,

Just exactly what did You have to do for Your Word to become flesh?

"Respectfully" Asking, Unbeliever,

For My Word to become Flesh

My Son was conceived

in the womb of a virgin

by My Spirit

on behalf Me

God—the Father.

XLIX

Wow, God! You dropped Your Son down through **a womb?**

Yep.

He was carried and birthed by one of Adam and Eve's daughters.

Ohhh. So that's how You beamed Him down to earth?

Yep. That's what joined My Son to her—as humanity's Son! Through His mother, My Son was made Flesh.

Dying Unbeliever,

I gave My Son to humanity!*

He is My Special Gift

That I wrapped in a Human Body

And sent to Earth

In "Earth-Suit" Attire

Carrying "Non-Contaminated"

PURIFYING

Human *Blood*

for Humanity's cleansing!

Since having pre-existed in Heaven

Before Arriving to the Earth

As *My Eternal Word*—

He would need a body.

So! For *My Eternal Word's*

Second Adamic *"Choosing" Experience*

I Added a **Newly** *"Deposited-for-the-Earth"*

"Able-to-Choose" **Human Will**

—Completely "Un"broken"

by Adam's Fall!

My Commission to Second Adam

—MY SON

Was "WORD--DO **MY Eternal WILL***

ON EARTH AS IT IS IN HEAVEN

—When You Land in Adam's Domain!

(Human comparison)

As with humanity—

*Ones word has **no** will!*

But O-N-L-Y speaks what

the possessor of the will—

*the **"will-holder"***

*—**speaker***

*Wants or **"wills"** to say*

(Now both heaven and earth terms)

By MY Design

*It is ones **w//Word***

that reveals

the thoughts

on the m/M of a s/Speaker!

*So, **AS DO I**—as Sovereign God...*

*Humanity—Think **before** you speak!*

*And certainly **before** you act!*

*For **BEST** words and actions*

*Come from **carefully "protected"***

thought

*that are closely **examined—and***

Reveal the work of a

*"**right**" mind*

*What Was On **MY Mind** in Heaven*

As the Father

—That I Willed and Carried Out

Through My WORD

On EARTH—

Was Adam's release!

*SO—I Sent My **Word***

AS THE ONLY WAY

To Provide **THE WAY**

for Humanity's Entrance

Back to ME!

And MY WORD—DID IT!!!

HE DID IT!

The TRUTH!

*MY **SOVEREIGN** TRUTH!*

DEFEATED

The Liar—

The author of sin

rebellion and death!

And through RESURRECTION POWER

WITH "SPIRIT Cleansing" BLOOD

Fueled by the Life of MY Spirit! My WORD—IN SPIRIT POWER! DEFEATED ETERNAL DEATH!!!

Dear God,

How'd You get to be **so** smart?

Where'd You learn **all-l** that?

Please keep typing 'cuz, I'm trying to get it!

P.S. Do you have any

"Basic God for Dummies" tips?

Dyi-ver,

This might help.

I Am the Governing Executive of OUR Community of ONE—that Exists in

Three Distint Parts—God the Father, God the Word, and God the Holy Spirit

But to Rescue Adam, Second Adam took on a Body—becoming My Son

But, still He and I Are ONE!*

Dyi-ver,

You—also—have your mind, your word and your spirit.

*And you are also **one** with your word—which represents what's on your mind!*

Any questions?

Ooo, Ooo!!! God,

I think I can get it if You'll go into my "comic-book" mode.

Okay, lil' Sport, I will.

Good—I'll close My eyes to go into comic-book "action" mode with You, God.

(God goes into "comic-book" Super-Hero "Will/Word" mode.)

"Agent *COMMANDER God the Father—"Dad"—To My Word—Do You copy?"*

"Yes Dad—I copy—what do You want Me to do?"

"My WILL"

*"Okay, Agent Commander Dad! What's on **Your Mind?**"*

"As Chief in Command, I want You to become Flesh to rescue fallen Adam!"

"Okay, Dad! But I'll need a Human Body—to Participate in Time."

"No problem, Son. Between Your mom to be, and Me, I'll give You

Humanity's Blood—for circulation in Your Veins—but uncontaminated and clean!

*And Son! You'll need a **Human will** to make Your Own "Human-choice" decision!*

'Cuz, just like Adam, Satan will try to trap You too—but I'm counting You—as My Word—to obey My Word—as My Son!!!"*

"10-4—Commander Dad! As Your Eternal Word—I will do Your Eternal Will*—and when Satan tries to make Me fall— with temptation—I will Speak Your Word!"

(Speaking from the "eternal future" to come.) "This is Heaven/ Earth Man—Word in Flesh—to the Chief Commander, saying Over and Out!!!!"

(Highly impressed) "Commander God!" That was a good one!

Thanks, Dyi-ver!

*The "comic-book" idea was a good one. There's just one last thing I'd like to cover before I close out My instruction. The way My Son carried My Power to earth to **Execute** My Will was...*

...[Excitedly interrupting God] 'Xcuse Me, God! But, I'll take over the instruction over from here!

50/50 God-Man ZO-O-O-OMS to the earth and says, **"Commander Dad, I made it! I loaded Myself up with plenty of Your POW-WOW Pow…"**

…Dyi-ver!

Focus! You don't even realize that you <u>just</u> interrupted Me! There was quite a bit more that I wanted to teach You about My Power. And by the way, Dyi-ver. **He's 100 Percent God 100 Percent Man!** *He's—My ETERNAL WORD—In a Human Body!!!!*

[The "Interrupting" Unbeliever does not pay attention.]

Note: The clarification that God the Father does not possess two Wills is important to the defense of Jesus' Diety, as God in the flesh. Some say Jesus and God cannot be One because One Entity cannot have Two Wills. (Jesus said, "I came to do the will of the Father.") To explain this: Father God "Willed" His Word (wrapped in a Body that possessed a Human will) to carry out His Heavenly Will, as a Man who came to humanity. Thus, Jesus, with a Human will, carried out the Father's Divine/Executive Will. As God's Eternal Word (a Member of God's Community of One, the Father, the Word and the Holy Spirit)—He, as God's Word did not possess the Will in the Triune Body. But as a Man, he had a Human body, Human blood—purely uncontaminated, **and** *a Human will. The Redeemer Second Adam carried out the Father's Eternal Will on earth, as the Eternal Son—through his* **unfallen/unbroken** *Human will.*

*Endnotes

L

[Out of nowhere, Dyi-ver starts loudly humming the Superman movie theme, and then blurts out...]

50/50 God-Man! Coming to theaters EVERYWHERE!

Dear God,

This concept would make a GREAT movie script! Half God and Half Man! I can see it now on the big screen!

There'd be Super-Hero music with Your Son leaping off a tall building—and then someone with a deep voice would bust outta nowhere sayin'...

"It's a bird!

It's a plane!

No, it's—"

—Rude Dyi-ver!

*Now, this is a PERFECT example of what you'd do in the class with that teacher who'd speak to Me about you **almost** every-single-day!!*

*There's a place for creativity, with a lively imagination, but not for **blurting out** right in the MIDDLE of class instruction! Now, I better understand why your teacher asked Me to take away her headache—**regularly!***

Dear God,

[Insulted] Sorry, but I don't think that's very funny!

Not funny! But, OH, so true!

Well, God. Since You brought that up, I do va-a-guely remember—.

You va-a-guely remember what, Dyi-ver?

What that teacher used to say to me! The one who used to talk to You about me **all** the time! You know, the one who I called **"Big Bertha"**!

[Recalling] Yep, Dyi-ver! Just <u>before</u> you got suspended!

Oh, yeah, I forgot about that!

Well, she said I'm too <u>easily</u> distracted and have ADHD!

No, Dyi-ver,

That was Dr. Brothers, the school psychologist!

Oh yeah, God!

That's right! I went to see ole' Dr. Brothers twice every week after school—second semester! So God, do you remember why I ended up getting suspended the **NEXT** time, and then the time **after** that?

Yes, Dyi-ver!

*It was for practicing your Spanish in **that teacher's** class!*

[Laughing] Oh—! You mean when I called her, **"Supercita Mama Grande?"**

"Suspended" Unbeliever,

Yep!

Oh, YES!

That's the day I found out that **"Mama Grande"** meant **"Big Mama"** in English!

No, Dyi-ver!

*That's the day you found out **your teacher meant BUSINESS**—in English!*

OH, brother!

No, it was Dr. Brothers.

Who did what, God?

*Who stopped her from getting you **expelled!***

OH—! Brother!

No, Dyi-ver,

*It was Dr. Brothers, the School Psychologist, **and ME!** We worked **very** hard, to keep you from getting COMPLETELY put out the District!*

Now settle down! Dyi-ver.

Remember Dr. Brothers said that you need to work on your—

[both God and Dyi-ver type at the same time]

Focus!

Yes-Sir-Ree-simo-desimo-stesimo,   God!   **Oh,   and "Euginio!"**

[Dyi-ver, having named close school friends, laughs in the pillow to try to keep God from hearing the delighted giggling about those school "d-aay-z."]

Dyi-ver,

*I can hear you! And by the way, it would be **100/100 God/ Man!** My Son Is **FULLY** God and **FULLY** Man. In fact, He's the "Resurrection Power Man!"* That would be a good name for your movie.*

*©E. E. Blessings 2019

*Now "Nodding" Dyi-ver," I'm **sure** You're ready for a little nap.*

LI

[Dyi-ver takes a little nod but wakes right back up.]

Dear God,

I'm too excited to sleep. I'm glad You like <u>my</u> movie idea.

Do You think we might be able to bank some money if "Resurrection Power Man" makes it to Hollywood?

Dear God,

I promise. I will share the money with You.

Dear Kind Dyi-ver,

*Thanks, but I don't need it! Up Here, the streets are paved with gold. But **showing folks that 100/100 God-Man res-urrected from the grave to bring humanity back to life**— ESPECIALLy in times like these—would be good for ALL the world to see!*

And they will!!! When My Son returns! The WHOLE WORLD will know!!

[Dyi-ver loves being called "kind" and excitedly buries face in the pillow to try to muffle the sound of "sleepy" but "very pleased" giggling.]

Dear God—,

Yes, "Sleepy" Dyi-ver?

You know sometimes when I'm extra tired I get really silly-z-z-z-z-z-z-z-z-z-z-z-z-z-z...

"Awake" God. 'xcuse me for *snoring z-z—z-z-Z-Z-Z-z-z--z-z-z-z...*

Sweet dreams, Snoring Dyi-ver!

[God puts in His ear-plugs.]

LII

Dear God!

Sorry for falling asleep on You. But it was great; I had such **sweet dreams!**

Dear Dyi-ver,

I know!

You already knew, God?

Yep! I spoke it!

Now, what's on your mind?

God,

Did I understand You correctly? Was one of my papa's daughters **re-a-lly** Your Son's mother?

Yep!

Well, what was her name?

Mary.

God, since she was my papa and mama's daughter, is she related to me?

"Related-to-Mary" Dyi-ver,

Yep. Because of Adam's "universal seed," all of humanity is "family" related. Thus, there is the "universal brotherhood/sisterhood of humanity."

And Mary is a full-fledged member of the human race.

Well, since she was Your Son's mother, that make her kinda special, right God?

Dear Dyi-ver,

*Despite that Mary was completely human, through her great faith and sacrificial willingness to carry My Son, she found special favor with Me! Thus, she was **highly blessed and favored among women.***

Well God,

With **all** her favor and blessing, wouldn't that have made her, as the Mother of God, somewhat *divine?*

Nope.

My Spirit overshadowed Mary in a unique way that was reserved only for her specially <u>chosen</u> experience. So, Mary was a full-human who had a fully-divine experience!

That said, generally, there are two errors regarding Mary's level of importance as the mother of humanity's Redeemer.

She is either uplifted to the status of deity, and that is too high— or reduced to commonality with every other woman—and that is far too low!

Mary had a human father and mother, but through the miracle-working power of My Spirit, she birthed My Son—who is Divine. He shed Heaven's Infinite, cleansing blood for ALL humanity, Mary not excluded, since...

...she was **also** touched by Adam's stain, God?

Yep. But her pure faith and "willing" availability for her "Divine" assignment so pleased Me.

Therefore, Mary will ALWAYS hold a special place in My Heart! Especially because it was through her that My Son became the Elder Brother of Adam.

And of particular significance to My appreciation for Mary was this: It was because of her that My Son, and those who have received Him, are able to join together in one-voice and pray, "Our Father" which art in Heaven..." speaking together to Me, the Heavenly Father. This prayer warms My Heart since it shows My DUAL Family relationship between My Only Begotten Son (Who came down from Heaven to earth—) and children of the earth who will come Upstairs to live with Me. As the Loving Father. I look forward to that quickly nearing day!

Dying Unbeliever,

Had it not been for the work of Mary and My Son, **Our** *Forever Family would have remained locked out of My Home Forever.*

Forever, God?

Forever...

LIII

[God speaks to all humanity in a slow, "Southern" drawl.].

HOWDY DO! Forevah Frienz, Unbelievahs and Lil' Dyi-vah.

How ya'll doin'?

Ya'll? Dear God!

Is that a **Southern** accent?

Yep! I love the South! Lil Dyi-!

["Dyi-vah" joins right in] But I thought You ONLY speak propah "Wes Coase," English. Arh You **from** the South, Mistah God?

*[Still speaking "Southern" and slowly] I tell you, Baby-Dyi-! That's what humanity tries tuh do—tie Me down to human limitations, based on Yo <u>finite</u> understanding of Me. But I **do not** confine myself to humanity's confining LIMITS.*

"I AM" that "I AM"!

I Exist Everywha'r…Omnipresent!

I have NO "start-time," and to My Reign, there will be NO END! I'll nevah die, Dyin' Unbelievah!

I Am the Eternally Existent!

Omnipotent…All Powerful!

Omniscient…All Knowin God!

[Taking questions from the World audience, now returned to regular Voice.]

I see the hand of the person in Australia. What is your question?

[Person steps up to the mic and asks a question.]

Why are there so many Mysteries that surround My Existence? Very good question. And by the way, I just love the Australian accent! (The speaker mirrors God's smile.)

*The Mysteries that surround My Eternal Existence are because I don't reveal ALL there is to know about Myself to **anyone, anywhere**…because, quite honestly human mind couldn't handle It! The "I AMness" of both Me **and** My Son has caused humanity to ponder deeply, without explanation, throughout time.*

[Looking toward North America]. The lady from the Talk Show! I'm so glad you're here. I've been thinking about you. You've been heavy on my mind!

Why Am I a Jealous God?

As the only Sovereign God—I'm Jealous for various reasons. First, let Me clarify. My Jealously is not defined by My irritation with the gifts and prestigue of those who work hard, and have earned—unless, of course, those gifts separate My beloved from Me. A mutually exclusive commitment between **only** *My Son, you, and Me eliminates the space for a "third-party's" involvement. For, as it is on earth—so it is in heaven, "the marriage love" of the groom is an exclusive commitment to only the bride; and an exclusive love from the groom is given in return.*

As Creator, I Am Jealous—not "of," but "for" the hearts of the people who I created to worship Me in spirit and in truth! I masterfully designed you to spend eternity with Me—as My child. And My Son is the ONLY God Who holds the authorization to insure your Eternal life in My Home. I Am committed **Only** *to Your Good. But, even the "well-intentioned," whose hearts divide away from Me must return, while there's still time.*

Adam was also unaware of the "jealous" intention of My enemy to divide hearts that love **only** *Me, away. He also did not know that a* **"buy-in"** *into the "additional god" option is a* **"buy-out"** *of Me. For I will be Lord of ALL, or I will not be Lord, at all! I love you, and it is more than Adam who My Son has given a Second Chance to return to Me.*

(The Son Speaks) "I don't mean to embarrass you, but will you marry me? For there is not a jealous bone in My Nail-Scarred Hands. I Am the Eternal Groom, and would love for you to be My bride."

The Son

SON,

Right here on LIVE National TV (Tel-the-vision!) You popped the BIG question! AMAZING! YOU ALWAYS Speak exactly what's on My Mind! I'm sure heaven's ratings went RIGHT through the SKY on that one!

LIV

Dyi-ver,

Words are humanity's mode of expression that indicates what someone desires, feels, accepts, rejects, etc.

Therefore, words are SO important! And that's why "receivers" must say, "I do" with their mouth, since My Son has proposed to humanity. You see... by one's words, one evidences their established "will"—their decision of the heart.

Dyi-ver,

In My Book to humanity, there is a section that says, "That if thou shalt confess with thy mouth (My Son), and shalt believe in thine heart that God hath raised him from the dead, thou shalt be saved."

Romans 10:9

"Saved"? Why is that important, God? I mean to **speak** "I'll accept Him"—**just** a couple words? How can that **"save"** anyone, or make **any** difference, for that matter?

Dear Dyi-ver "Speaker-of-Words-that-Express-Your-Will!"

*"Lord, I receive You as My Lord and Savior. Come into My life," is a **great** confession. And while those words spoken might appear insignificant, they are **deeply** significant because they express the commitment of one's will and one's heart to receive My Son. And then the next step is to become a follower who follows closely—.*

Dear Dyi-ver,

Gathering in My House on earth is a great way to follow closely, and it helps keep My children from looking back.

Dear God,

You have a House on earth?

Yep. It's the church. The one I speak of now is the "brick and mortar" church (for the body of every believer is also My dwelling place, and there is the invisible church built on the Rock—My Son.) Dyi-ver, the church is v-e-r-y important to Me. And the way to know if it's really My House, is if they speak My Word, as written in the Book I sent to humanity for its guidance—without compromise!

So, Dying Unbeliever,

Confess My SON, as My Saving Word!

Meditate on Him, as My Written Word!

Honor Him, as My Living Word!

Accept Him, as MY CLEANSING Word!

And

Speak Him, as My DELIVERING Word!

Dear God,

There might be something to the "Power of the Word," because it was DEFINITELY **MY** word that got **ME** in trouble in Big Mama Grande's class! But, God, I meant EVERY last word that I said to her! That teacher got on my **LAST** nerve!

*Suspended **AGAIN** Unbeliever,*

She sure did!

And that LAST word, is why you missed the LAST day of school!

Well, *my* word!!! OUCH!

LV

Dear God,

When I got home "the day of" the little run in, I got the Board of Education put on my Seat of Knowledge!

By my dad—the resident "superintendent" of school!

Crying Unbeliever,

Oh, I was there.

God,

That was SO irritating. On that one, **both** my parents let my brothers and my sister get away with laughing!

Jumping Dyi-ver,

I'm pretty sure it was because of how high you were jumping to miss those "three" swats your dad laid out, very strategically! To tell the truth, your acrobatics that day were quite unique!

As were those three swats! Oh brother. I'm sure that's why I don't like ping-pong paddles to **this** day. My father said "the paddlin'" was because he loved me, but my brother said it was because of **what** I said.

Dyi-ver,

*What I recall is that it was **highly effective**. You **never** had a problem with your teacher a day after your father provided that "ping pong paddle" therapy. In fact, that dose made My job **a lot** easier. After getting your father involved, the next school year, your teacher didn't hardly speak to Me at ALL—about you.*

[Smiling at a sweet memory] Dear God,

While we're on my father, this is a good time for me to get a small point of clarification about something I find confusing about You and Your Son.

What is it, Dyi-ver?

Well, God. On earth a father and his son are two separate individuals—**not one** combined Unit. Yet, You say—You, as the **Father** and Your Word, as Your **Son**—are ONE? What's the deal?

Great question, Thinking Dyi-ver! Two things,

*When, I sent My Son to the earth, I paralleled Our roles as Father and Son to the father and son model I established with **Adam and his sons**. However, there was ONE eternal distinction that existed in My unique relationship between **My** Son and Me.*

Dear God,

What was the distinction?

*The fathers and sons of humanity are separate individuals, and thus have separate birthdates, (which indicates their separate, individual dates of their times of arrival to the earth.) Even if a father and son share **the same** birthday month and day, the event of each birth occurred in a different birth year. The father is always older.*

But when My Son came to earth, having been born of Mary, despite having an "arriving birth date" to the earth, He still maintained His Eternally Distinct Status, as My Eternal Word from Heaven—where He is from Everlasting. So, while receiving a date of birth on earth—His mother's side, Eternal Birth Records on My End showed NO date of birth. What explains this is that, as His Heavenly Father, I Am the Everlasting Existent One—since never Born. Thus on My Side—as My Eternal Word—My Son IS the Eternally Existent One, TOO. In fact,

My Son caused quite a stir when He stated to a group, concerning Himself, "Before Abraham was—I AM."*They were fit to be tied because the people knew He was declaring Himself to be God. That night when He prayed, He told Me all about it, I just laughed because the joke was NOT on My Son!

Dying Unbeliever,

*It's an Amazing Experience, that to rescue humanity, now, I, **too** have a Son!*

*Endnotes

LVI

Dear God,

Being **together eternally** is a long time. So, did the Two of You **ever** separate?

Dear Dying Unbeliever,

We did separate once.

*When My Son died on the Cross, He experienced death, and it was the **first and only** time We separated.* As the Father, **I left Him alone** just long enough for Him to be touched by Adam's Sin and humanity's death. For He came to earth, as the Perfect Lamb I prepared for humanity's Sacrifice to be Slain!*

But, why God? Why would You let Your Son suffer like that?

"Caring" Dyi-ver,

*He bore the wrath I felt for Adam's rebellion. "Care" for My Son that would prevent His suffering and death would have been "death" for ALL humanity—a **HUGE victory** for My enemy—and devastating Loss for Me. IN THIS SPIRITUAL WAR, that **was not** an option! For my Son had to experience NOT only*

Adams physical death—the cessation of a heart beat, pulse beat, physical breathing, etc—But He also had to experience Adam's spiritual death—Spiritual Separation from Me—the Father! And separate We did!

*As the Father, I Am **so** grateful that My Son Is equipped, and was **willing** to War on My behalf. And since His little brother's rescue was a Job, not for the Father, but for the Word, My Son handled business quickly!*

*Endnotes

LVII

Dear God,

Exactly what did Your Son do when He got into the ring with Death?

Glad you asked, Dyi-ver! Because this is the EXCITING part!

(Announcer) ROUND 1! Ding!!!

When My Son entered the Ring, Death took His body down. **But this was a set-up!** *It was a War maneuver on Our end. I knew in order for My Son to access the grave—to conquer death and loose the imprisoned—He would have to take a "death BLOW" first!*

So the Attack Plan was that My Son's Body would be brought down under the power of death, but not for long! On Day 3!!!

(Announcer) Final Round—3! Ding! Ding! Ding!!!

The Third Day—He would RISE UP—AND CRUSH death by the Power of My Word—which carries the Potent Power of My Spirit!!!

*Yep. That was Our Strategy, and **here's** what happened. My Son confronted Satan, Personally—unexpectedly—and made His DEMAND—THROUGH THE GRAVE!*

"HAND ME YOUR KEYS! UNLOCK THE CHAINS OF DEATH THAT'VE BEEN HOLDING MY FATHER'S CHILDREN IN YOUR DEADLY PRISON CHAINED AND BOUND! AND I MEAN LET THEM GO NOW!!!!!!!"

(Announcer) T-K-O!!! Triumphant Knock Out!!!!!!

"Announcer" and the boxing ring idea courtesy of Lily N. Richardson - 2020

LVIII

*Satan started **MOVING!** He unloosed the chains that held Adam and Eve! Abraham! Moses! Noah! Samson! Mary! Naomi and Ruth! AND **ALL** those who had died in the FAITH! They'd been imprisoned long enough! And each and every one of them ran out to their Eternal Freedom with joy, when My Son loosed the prison doors!*

Job came out with both hands lifted up, praising! "I told you my Redeemer liveth! He said—DEATH—I'M OUT!"*

Those who died in the faith were AMAZED. My Son escorted ALL of them OUT of Satan's Eternal Possession, and they have not been back since!

Prisoners UNCHAINED! SET FREE.

But the grave tried to block MY SON! And there was an ETERNAL RUMBLE!! It was DEATH! AGAINST MY WORD!

*Death **toppled** My Son's Body with a Deadly Right Hook. BUT MY SON IS A SKILLED FIGHTER! So, compared to what He did to death, what happened to Him was just a minor wound!*

*My Son **completely** broke death's power, and then…*

…HE CRUSHED THE DEVIL'S HEAD!!!*

Dyi-ver!

HE WAS HEATED!

MY SON GAVE DEATH A FIRST-CLASS BEAT DOWN!!!!!!

And My Son couldn't wait to tell ME about It!

WOW, God. That was rough AND tough! like SUPE MAN!!!

*Endnotes

LIX

Wait—Wait, Dyi-ver!

Here's the best part! Being Hit by Death for three days, My Son didn't like It! He felt what Satan had put Adam through, and as Adam's Big Brother, He BUSTED THE GRAVE WIDE OPEN!!!

With RESURRECTION POWER—My Son **H-I-T** ADAM'S DEATH WITH AN ETERNAL BLOW THAT WAS FELT THROUGHOUT TIME AND ETERNITY!

BOOM! POW! POW! YIKES! CA-B-O-O-OM!

DYI-VER!!!

I'MA tell you—MY SON WRESTLED THE LIFE OUT OF ETERNAL DEATH! AND SLAPPED IT ONE LAST TIME BEFORE LEAVING!

MUCH FASTER THAN THAT SPEEDING BULLET! HE BUSTED OUT OF THE GRAVE,

HE GOT UP—DYI-VER!

WITH **ALL** POWER IN HIS HANDS!

I'm telling You, Dyi-ver, My Son was movin' so FAST, until humanity's Rescue didn't take Him long, at all!

*AND IN JUST A **FEW** DAYS, HE WAS BACK UP HERE WITH ME IN HIS GLORIFIED RESURRECTED, BODY!!!**

Really, I guess some might see this as bragging, but I see it as just REMINISCING, Dyi-ver!

*Now, I call Him "The Death Defeater" and He **loves it!***

Whew! Now, let Me calm down!

"Angels, May I have some Living Water, Please."

*After the Lore Jesus had spoken to them, He was taken up into heaven and sat down at the right hand of God. Mark 16:19

LX

Dear God,

Are You, okay?

Yep. Just, let me catch My breath! I got caught up in the Greatest Story ever told.

It was a GOOD one—God!

So—I'm curious. Did Your Word die in that Fight?

NOPE!

*Heaven and earth shall pass away, but My Word shall **stand forever.*** So, while His "earthen body" died, the Power in My Word is what got My Son UP ALIVE!*

My Word is Spirit, and it is Life!**

And know this, Dyi-ver!

Because of this, as God, the Father, I was fully confident that My Son would come through His death, and Our separation

253

*with glaring success because I know what He knows—**THERE IS RESURECTION LIFE IN THE WORD!** So, AS MY WORD—My Son lit into Death with **full** "Word Confidence!"*

Yep. My Son's Body went down, but…

I did not die!

My Spirit did not die—and

My Word—did not die.

*My Eternal Word and I separated briefly, since I could not accompany My Son into the experience of death, due to sin. But when My Son rangled with Death—in little to no time, My Son was back! And by the time I cleared My throat, I had gotten **"MY Word"** back. And He got UP with ALL POWER over not only life, but NOW—ETERNAL DEATH—in His Hands!*

DYI-VER,

*MY SON GOT UP WITH **A-L-L** POWER IN HIS HANDS!*

Dying Unbeliever,

My Son suffered A LOT in that PAINFUL EXPERIENCE, but He made it through!

Dear God,

Really! But it seems SO unfair that He had to endure ALL that PAIN in His Fight.

Dying Unbeliever,

There are several billion…trillion reasons why He went through it. It's called winning the lost at ANY cost.

Precious Unbeliever,

Dying souls are precious gifts worth fighting for—one freed life at a time.

*Heaven and earth shall pass away, but my words shall not pass away. Matthew 24:35

**The words that I speak unto you, they are spirit, and they are life." John 6:63

LXI

Speaking of **precious gifts!**

Dear God,

[Deeply concerned] I'm hoping Your Baby Son had at least o-n-e birthday party since He came down to help my poor ole' papa! I hope he got at *least* one present at a birthday party on His mother's side.

Dear Christmas Dyi-ver,

Have you ever gotten a Christmas present?

Oh Wow! My red bicycle that I *sneaked* and opened on Christmas Eve was My **best** Christmas present EVER!

Sneaky Dyi-ver,

*Christmas is My Son's **special** Gift to you!*

Dear Dyi-ver,

It was a Silent Night.

LXII

"For unto (humanity) a child is born, and unto (humanity) a Son is given."*

That Night on the Cross!

[Both God and the Dying Unbeliever type at the same time]

It was a Bloody night!!! (The Dying Unbeliever)

It was a Holy night!!! (God)

*For unto us a child is born, unto us a son is given. Isaiah 9:6

LXIII

Dear God,

Original dad was responsible for Your Son going through a lot, God!

[Silence]

Dear Dyi-ver,

—a whole lot!

[Awkward silence, so the Dying Unbeliever quickly changes the subject.].

LXIV

Dear God,

I've thought about it, and You must be <u>quite</u> proud of Your Son!

Dyi-ver,

I really am. He's a great Son—represented Me on the earth for 33 years, and then He took a cloud and came right back Home after He finished His Work. I'll always remember when He came and sat down on My right hand. I must admit, that was a moving moment for Me!

He's such an Outstanding Young Man—fully God! While on earth, He showed the world Who I Am! And He has ALL My traits, (not to take away from His mother. She helped Him become a contributing citizen to humanity.)

*I don't mean to go on boasting, but My Son's My Spittin' Image! When anyone in the earth saw Him, they saw Me! I Am a **very** Proud Father, indeed!*

Oh, Dyi-ver,

And He was the Special Delivery Package! But, I'll tell you more about that in the next chapter!

Dear God,

The next chapter? What does that mean?

Oh, that's right, Dyi-ver, you don't know about the book!

The book? Dear God,

Am **I** in it?

LXV

Special Delivery!

Excuse me for just a minute, God. But I think someone **just** sent me a Special Delivery! Maybe it's the book! How EXCITING!

*No, Dyi-ver. It was **THE** Special Delivery.*

THE what, God?

The Special Delivery!

Dyi-ver,

Have you ever heard of the word, "anthropomorphism"?

Yes! I loved English!

Yep, Dyi-ver, that you did!

Anthropomorphism?

Dear God,

Now let's see. Major **big** word! That's…

A-n-t-h-r-o-p-o-m-o-r-p-h-i-s-m

Yep. And you spelled it correctly, too.

Great. Let me pull it up on my computer. Got it! It's giving human traits and emotions to a *non-human* entity.

Very good, Dyi-ver!

Thanks, God! But what does "anthropomorphism" have to do with the price of tea in China?

Well—smarty pants—let Me tell You about My Son's virgin birth.

Dear God,

Your Son was born of **a virgin?**

*Yes, Dyi-ver, **the** virgin!*

Dear God,

T-h-e virgin? Now—You have my **f-u-l-l attention**! And I PROMISE, I will <u>focus</u>.

FULL attention? You'll focus, Dyi-ver? Best promise I've gotten from you in a lonnnng time!

(Typed quiety to try to "dodge" God's hearing) **Oh** brother!

*Oh, Dyi-ver! Ummm... I'm thinking this whole "Special Delivery" transaction **really** should be listed in the Guinness Book of World's Records.*

Why, God?

Because, Dyi-ver,

It was the ONLY Miraculous Artificial Insemination Surgery in the intersection of heaven AND earth's history! And that's an AMAZING fact!

LXVI

⌘

(Unimpressed) Just a sec God, let's make sure we're on the **same** page.

Artificial insemination? You mean where a man's seed is sent into a woman's womb? Not through the regular process of intercourse, but through a **scientific process** of injection?

Y-E-S-S-S!!! But Dyi-ver,

*A miracle transcends science. In MY Miracle—I went F-A-R **beyond** science in the Transmission of My Seed from heaven to earth—into the chosen earthen vessel! This transmission was done through the Power of My Spirit! The Holy Spirit deposited My Life-Giving Blood—void of Adam's death—into Mary's womb, initiating the Miraculous Conception of My Only Begotten Son.*

Well, that does sound f-a-i-r-ly impressive, God.

Ya think? (Carrying on) Especially significant to My Son's birth is that My Cleansing Blood, delivered into Mary's womb, carries My

Genetic coding of "Everlasting-Life." Its importance to humanity is that it carries "Life-Cleansing" Additives, which factor into the new-births of My "non-biological," but "spiritual" children.

Dear God,

So basically, Your Son's birth was somewhat a result of of a Miraculous "Artificial Insemination—anthropomorphism" Combo! In this case, mother Mary carries Your Child Fathered by the Power of Your Spirit?) Fairly Miraculous, God!

Well "fairly" thank you, Dyi-ver. Since it took a God/human birth—to create a God/Man, then I had to come up with a Workable Plan for all parties involved.

*You are absolutely correct. I did not complete the actual "deed" of a man. But, through the Power of My Spirit, Mary conceived. And I "Begot" the DUAL-Layered "Son of God **and** Son of Man." To free enslaved Adam—as Second Adam—through My Power! What a Purpose!*

Oh, that IS right! Poor ole' **"slave-trade"** dad needed to be freed!

***"Need to be Freed"** Dyi-ver,*

My Son came through a Special Delivery to deliver humanity great HOPE!

LXVII

Oh, Dear!

*God! You just reminded me that I'm pretty sure papa's FILTHY stain is **STILL** on me!*

<u>*Are you serious?*</u>

Dear God!

This is somewhat **irritating!** I wonder if my papa **permanently** stained me for the **rest** of my life!!!? (Falls back landing a "bed-thud!") Note to self: I need to find out if the doctor has something for a chronic case of the "Adamic nature" that may be worsening?

Chronic Case of Negative Dyi-ver!

That's *your take-away from My Son's HOPE? With all our "life-giving" chats, you're focus is **still** on the first Adam's LOSS, rather than the Second Adam's GAIN?*

"Stuck" Unbeliever,

After ALL our conversations about VICTORY, **how on earth** *did you* **still** *end up focused on Adam's problem?*

Well, I promised I would focus, God—but I didn't say on what!

By the way, God...

Now, I'm wonderin' if **that might** explain why my Adamic nature keeps showing up. I still have my papa's ole STAIN, and a **lot** of his "slave-trade" habits!

("Stuck" glancin') In 4th grade, I had to go to the end of the line for cutting—at least 12 times! In 5th grade, I almost got COMPLETELY kicked outta school. Twice I was busted for tying my best friend's shoe-laces together. (Nap-time— Kindergarten, back in the day.) And when my pet mouse climbed outta that box and crawled on the "Mama's" chair— Dr. Brother's said, **I'm** the one who had the ADHD!!?? (What gives, God?) We BOTH know it was My teacher who did **ALL** the jumpen'!!!)

In fact, come to think of it, I think there's a lot of other stuff that got passed down to me from "fig-leaf" pops! And right now this bent toward ir-ri-tation and complaining **tops** my "Adam had'm" list!

[Clears throat preparing to sing "the 'Adamic nature' blues."] Umh, Umh, Umh.

'Xcuse Me, God, but I feel a complaint comin' on NOW!

"III'VVVVEEE BEEN TROUGH IT ALL!"

"POOOOR OLE' ME!!!"

Off-key Dyi-ver,

Don't you hit another off-key note!

*Some of your "stuff" **d-i-d** come from Adam—but, more and more it's starting to look like quite a bit of your **BAGGAGE** is a more **recent** load!*

*Every time you sound like you're FINALLY starting to move in a **changed-life** direction—you come <u>clear</u> out of **left field** **with—a buncha foolishness...**and **now** you won't let go of the past!*

Really, Dyi-ver!

*I don't recall you being filled with **t-h-i-s** much negativity as a child!*

Dear God,

I was **born** this way—!

Well—"Adam-Born" Unbeliever!

*You need to be **born again!***

*You need **a** good dose of **"God"** Power…*

—Yes, God?

*…**e-a-c-h** day!!*

"No-Power" *Dyi-ver,*

You need to "pray-pray!"

LXVIII

[Typing quietly, hoping God won't hear.].

Well gee thanks, papa! Now that I think about it, it WAS my Adamic nature that got me in so much trouble in school!

And sent numerous times to the "focus" corner where I almost got a permanent seat!

Like…Real-ly! I was born this way!

And now God is saying that I need to be **born again!**

A new birth—NOW? I don't think so!

Good grief, dad! Long time ago, He said I look just like you! And, now I think I'm starting to s-e-e it!

Daring choices! A poor appetite, AND difficulty following clear instructions!

I'm pretty sure **YOUR** fall explains why **my health is broken, too!** Shat-tered genes!

THANKS DAD!

(Cuts in) Blaming Unbeliever,

*That's how you inherited the **blaming** gene—Adam blamed Eve, Eve blamed the serpent. And it's the serpent that deceived.*

*But My Son came, Dyi-ver, and you **must** receive!*

LXIX

Dearest Dying Unbeliever,

The message I gave to the world applies to you!

*"For God so loved the world that He **gave** His only begotten Son that **whosoever believeth in Him** should not perish, but have everlasting life."*

John 3:16

I did not send My Son to <u>SAVE</u> the whole world, but to give the dying world an alternative eternal option that's—available to ALL—if chosen.

"Alternative" Path-Taker,

Walk wisely…because I want You to be My child!

Please, God,

I hope you can understand that all of this gets sorta confusing. There's so many voices in the world!

I know, Seeking Unbeliever.

But the sheep hear the Shepherd's Voice, and a stranger's voice they will not follow.

John 10: 4, 5

Unbeliever "In Stranger-Danger!!!"

*The Good Shepherd is My Son, but there **IS** humanity's foe.*

Dear God,

But what about those who have **already** heeded to the voice of the stranger? What about them?

It is they who must choose—to heed the voice of My Word. And—return while there's still time!

And there is still time

But, know this—Delaying Unbeliever—time is winding down!

So I say unto one, and I say unto all—return quickly! Confessing "one-returning" decision-at-a-time.

*For My Son offers **no** "Universal Choice Plan"—and there is **no** "universal reconnection" in Me!*

LXX

God,

But what about the **other** gods? WHY can't they count?

So many of them have earned the trust of the masses of the earth, promising eternal life—but on paths that deviate from Your Son's!

Honorable gods! That's what they're called, and that's why they're worshipped so readily!

Oh, **dear** God!

What about them?

LXXI

Dying Unbeliever,

I have only **One** Begotten Son Who I sent to earth from Heaven, through a virgin birth.

And I have no **illegitimate** children!

A lesser god exists as a member of the fallen god's family, and thus is not in Mine.

A lesser god, created by stained hands, like its creator—is stained, too!

And a god born of a "stained" earthly father released from a mother's womb, **also** is stained and fallen—and therefore, cannot Redeem.

The gods concocted in the minds of darkened imaginations were birthed through unrepentant minds—and thus, wander in darkeness, too.

And those who serve them—as, the still fallen—must be lifted UP through the Finished Work of the Resurrected, Resurrecting One!—The LIFTER!

LXXII

Just Your Son, and none other?

Oh, God,

This is such an **un-embracing,** intolerant point of view!

"Intolerant" Unbeliever,

Exactly!

A loving parent will not tolerate it!

They will not "embrace" the consumption of anything that will lead to the death of one of their misguided children. That's called **intelligent intolerance,** *and it's VERY Parental!*

Loved One,

I Am the Omnicient, All-knowing Parent. I understand that **the lesser** *gods that remain outside of My Son—and each member of humanity who* **still** *resides in them—upon their entry into eternity—will be in eternal violation of Section 3:16* of My Eternal Life Policy! And* **thus,** *while standing on eternal sinking sand, will have no "sinking-sand" Policy coverage!*

*For God so loved the world, that he gave his only begotten Son, that whosoever believeth in him should not perish, but have everlasting life. John 3:16

As in **Q**

    U

    I

    C

    K

    S

    A

    N

    D

    God?

"Sinking-Quickly" Unbeliever…

Yep.

Oh—h—Dear! That CAN'T BE GOOD!

LXXIII

But God!!

What you are saying is **so** hard! Millions have come **to love other gods for a million individual reasons!**

And to speak candidly, it seems as if You won't take into consideration humanity's need for something familiar!!

God,

You keep pointing me to Your Son, and He's Someone I don't even know—we've never met before.

But I do know this! He landed on a Cross that didn't add up to a "comfortable stay" while "dropping in" on us down here for a while. And it sound's like He went out the hard way.

Even as His Dad, You've acknowledged His Cross experience was **bloody! But, was anything ever done about it?**

So—after listening to Your spiel, I'm starting to question why Your Son's death was never reported as a Human-Rights violation. Let's just face it! He got NAILED!!!

Add to that, His Bio—I've been told that it reads:"Lied on! Rejected. Mistreated for no good reason, AND whipped up a hill?"

"Good Heavens!"

A-l-s-o, I've been thinking, God! Are You ABSOLUTELY sure Your Son died for humanity—**willingly?** Or might He have felt **unduly pressured?**

I mean just slightly…to come down here to help out His little brother—!

I'm just about sure when He looked down, my papa was probably looking **rea-lly** pitiful, haven' fallen into such an embarrassing position.

I mean what else could explain ANYONE swapping a Mansion for a chance to give blood? REALLY?

And my **f-i-i-i-nal point,** God!

I'm starting to wonder if Your Son left heaven **will-ing-ly,** or did He get **PUSHED?**

LXXIV

Conspiracy Thinker!

*It was for the **joy** that was set before Him that My Son endured the Cross, **despising the shame!***

Hebrews 12:2

My point exactly! SHAME!

Dear God,

I don't fully understand the meaning of what you just typed, but I DO know it includes the word *"SHAME"*! And, not braggen," but I've studied a little Latin, a little Greek **and** some French, and I know that *SHAME* means *SHAME!*

And Your Son, as a *Grown Man* being referred to as **"a Sacrificial Lamb??"** I'm gonna just leave that part alone!

Think about it, God!

Getten' Hung Up, Strung Up, Beat Up and **a-l-l** folks talk about Is how **good** everything ended UP?

Hel-lo! **Reeeeeeeal pain!** But the "Forever Family Crew???" Oh, no!!! They just keepa singin' and a celebratin' that after He was Hung Up—He **still** got UP!

But, what about Him gettin' BANGED UP?? OH! And let's not forget about "bailed-out" papa!!! Broke outtah prison scott-free on the blood of an Innocent Man, and SOMEONE dropped the charges!!! Case dismissed!

Knock Knock—who's in chains? Oh-h-h—no one who **"CHOOSES"** to escape because Somebody ELSE got **Killed?**

Is it just **me,** or is something **way wrong** with that **get outta jail FREE Picture?**

LXXV

⤜∽⤛

*Dear **Protesting** Unbeliever,*

*You protest so **recklessly** because you've **never** been bound in the prison of hopeless death!*

*My Son shared—**Personally**—in Adam's deth experience—and He wants to keep humanity out!!!*

"Yes!" His death was horrific!

But it was ALSO necessary.

It was merciful.

It was useful.

__And it WAS willful!__

He suffered, bled and died not only for humanity.

But—He did it for Me!

"Unrelated" Unbeliever,

__I wanted a Family to call My OWN!__

LXXVI

[Silence]

Dear God,

I know my time is running out, but before I make my final decision I must get a definite answer to **this** question.

What was original mom doing when papa took the **bite?**

Oh, she was busy talking!

Oh! It figures!

Well, was it something **she** said that helped get poor ole' pops in **all** his trouble?

Dyi-ver. It was!

Good grief!

Great—Grief!

I gave Adam a command that he disobeyed—while listening to Eve—who was deceived by the Deceiver—the one who lies!

So, God, does Your enemy **still** lie to people today?

Dying Unbeliever,

Right now—he's lying to you!

LXXVII

Dear God'

I cannot accept it!

Unaccepting Non-believer,

You cannot accept what?

Any of it! I cannot accept the Cross and all the *bloody* stuff! Such a **painful death!** It *really* bothers me that all this was strictly unnecessary—**totally** uncalled for.

*Totally uncalled for? Dying Unbeliever! What do you **mean?** Which part of IT?*

A-L-L of IT, God!

THE WHOLE DEAD ENCHILADA! Because quite frankly, it seems like **my papa** made a BIG "death-mess," and **Your Son** did all h-i-s clean-up work!

*Ungrateful Unbeliever, My Son <u>did</u> do **ALL of Adam's Clean-Up Work!***

My point, exactly! **So,** God! Logi-cal-ly speaking… Just a **lit-tle** l-o-g-i-c around here would help! Just **one** ounce of good reasoning would show that it was **my-y dad! And not Your-r-r Son** who should've died!

And while the **"love" stuff** is good, it seems downright unfair that Your Son came **al-l** the way from heaven down, and ended up losing just about **al-l** His human *dignity hanging on a Tree!*

"Dignified" Dying Unbeliever!

*But a father's love—**the** Father's love—**transcends** human logic! The transaction of the Cross was driven by **MY** love!*

Yes, God! You did the loven' but it was Your **Son** who did all the dyen'!

Dying Unbeliever!

*The justice of God is greater than the fairness of life! I **cancelled** the Sin-Debt against humanity with every **nail** that WOUNDED My Son on the Cross!*

And what WOUNDS My Son WOUNDS Me!!!

LXXVIII

Dear God,

I have listened—I have made my decision, and it is **final!** I **can-not** accept Your Son's charity that **so** unfairly took His life!

So sorry, God—divine justice is important to *You*. But human justice and the preservation of human dignity is HUGE to *me!* Your Son's human side deserved a <u>**better**</u> **break!**

Broken Unbeliever,

My Son's break was that He was broken for YOU! To satisfy **My WRATH against Adam's rebelling betrayal**—so that **MY JUSTICE** would not be compromised—HE DIED. And, what is HUGE is that you have missed the WHOLE point!

Oh, I got the point, God! It was papa's irresponsible "Free Will Fruit Feast-Fest" that led to Your Innocent Son's death!

You see God, **I'm** big on everyone taking ownership of their **"o-w-n"** stuff.

So this "Innocent-Third-Party-paid-it-all-so-**case dismissed"** stuff doesn't sit well with me!

Consequently—as a responsible child in this dysfunctional family matter, I want to separate myself from ANYTHING that has to do with my dad's bill being "paid-in-full" by Someone who I don't e-ven know. "A family freebee?" I hope I'm above that!

So for that reason—I'm out!

Dying Unbeliever!

*Are you sure you want to commit to **that** position? Is that really how you feel?*

LXXIX

Dear God,

That's **exactly** how I feel! So, having already expressed appreciation for Your Son's generosity, I still think He's quite an admirable Man, but my family's debt problem clearly was not His obligation!

And while I really don't like airing my family's dirty laundry, I'm convinced my dad was **very** wrong for making a debt he could not pay, and leaving Your Son to pay a debt He did not owe!

Papa's debt **c-l-e-a-r-l-y** was not Your Son's responsibility!!!

And with all due respect, I don't think Your Son should've had to pay it! In fact to be completely honest God, I don't think humanity even needed Your Son to clear up its debt problem—in the first place!

Because I know my family. We might not be perfect, but when it comes right down to it, and we're forced to take charge, we can get just about ANY job done between ourselves. And to tell the truth, quite a few of us do excellent work!!

And by the way, God!

Yes, there IS trouble in the world, but what about humanity's GREAT accomplishments?

I don't think You've acknowledged ANY of that! What about our education, science, technology, and not to speak of our space travel (that by the way is getting <u>a lot</u> closer to coming up near to You,) and our superb entertainment!

A-N-D! Have you EVER stopped to notice how nicely we display OUR notable **accomplishments** on the World Wide Web?

LXXX

〰

[God ponders quietly, deeply reflecting on matters, but remains silent in His thoughts. The Dying Unbeliever, with feelings of unparalleled human greatness, types on—until finally God speaks!]

Dear "Self-Important" **Dying** *Unbeliever!*

I created humanity in My image, and so humanity also creates. When the work of My Hands—is touched by the work of humanity's added creativity—miracles in the form of great accomplishments do materialize! But My gifts are not given for humanity to enjoy materialism and forget Me!

Yes, the evidence of the dominion over the earth that I gave to humanity, through Adam, is profound. But the evidence that the earth has been touched by the corruption of Adam's Stain is quickly becoming much more profound.

Consequently, so often at the core of humanity's glamour stories and images, and its power and prestige, is the seething of human jealousy, pride, and the viciousness that comes with competing, conflict, and opposing self-interests.

As a result, the World Wide Web of which you boast, so frequently reports humanity's **World Wide violence, World Wide disease, World Wide perplexities—to the World-Wide confused who are deeply troubled—World Wide!**

Humanity. Remember Now thy Creator…For there is no word in the human vernacular that properly describes the "Eternal Nothingness" of the ETERNAL UNREPENTANT locked in ETERNAL DEATH!

Concept taken from words inspired by Oracia Y. McCurtis - 2019

Remember now thy Creator in the days of thy youth, while the evil days come not, nor the years draw nigh, when thou shalt say, I have no pleasure in them.

Ecclesiastes 12:1

LXXXI

[Ignores God and keeps feverishly typing.]

But by now I think You might've noticed that despite Your opinion about my family, humanity has been <u>hugely</u> success-ful in redeeming ourselves in **numerous** ways!

Dear God,

We are the world,

We are the children,

We are the ones who make a better life when we start giving!

There's a choice we're making,

We're saving our own lives,

It's true We'll make a better World if we *just believe!*

Lyrics from "We Are the World" by Michael Jackson and Lionel Richie (1985)

Dying Unbeliever,

Believe in what?

Believe in <u>ourselves</u>! Because—

God!

The family of humanity is quite a bit on its own—pardon Me, but even <u>without</u> Your Son!

Dying Unbeliever,

*Is that **really** what you think?*

Oh yes, God!

And I genuinely feel it would be *such* a tribute to my family, as a people, if we could do something to return Your Son's "debt-payment" back to Him—in full, one good deed at a time!

I sincerely believe we as humanity have **earned** the right to pay off our **own** debt! Because we have already restored so much of the human dignity we lost in Adam.

Personal redemption! Through o-u-r own good works, not the Blood of a Son Who You refer to as humanity's Sacrificial Lamb. **That's the politically correct answer!** So it's the family's RIGHT—to do with or without Him.

And there's quite a few of us who just don't want Him involved in our affairs! **O-kay?**

LXXXII

Your words are foolish—Disrespectful Unbeliever!

They are not wise! People try that every day—to eliminate My Son. But a Fierce Roaring Lion **can't** *be dismissed.*

Yes. He came to earth showing His "Lamb's" side—Gentle, Sacrificed, and Slain. But—"The Lion" has Risen as KING.* And in Kingly Ferociousness, as the Family Protector of His Father's pride—He waits in Stately Position. POSTURED TO POUNCE—to devour those who tried to devour Him— ROARING!!! He Sits ready to ATTACK!!! Sending Everlasting shock to those who **attack** *Him.*

HE IS the Lion of the tribe of Judah—the root of David—and HE HATH PREVAILED!

But we have talked enough, Dying Unbeliever. You who have rejected My Son! Enter thou now into My domain!

LXXXIII

Oh, this is SO frustrating! Hello, can anybody hear me? Hello, can anybody HELP ME? Why does the response generated keep coming up ACCESS DENIED?

Hello! Is there an attendant on duty? I'm trying to get through heaven's gates. I'm a new arrival!

Help! PLEASE! I'm out here, and it's getting really hot! The heat is coming closer, and I'm trying to get in!

Can someone help me reach God? PL-EASE!

Who are you?

Oh, I'm the Dying Unbeliever. Thank God I finally got through!

Oh no, you have not gotten through these gates! My Father's house is not open to you!

This conversation is now terminated. You have been assigned to a different eternal address!

My Father's house is not your home!

NO! Please! Wait! Your Father and I are friends!

Check with Him. We were just talking via email.

He'll recognize who I am and I'm sure He'd want You to let me in! I'm pretty sure He's expecting me!

And I know He wouldn't want You to make this **SO** uncomfortable!

Oh, you're the one who's trying to come to My Father, and bypass Me? It doesn't work that way up Here!

Oh, You must be God's Eternal Son?

*Yes, I Am! Depart from Me. This is no place for a stranger!!! I never knew, you—so, leave—unwashed one, with the stains of My Father's enemy **still** on you! I can smell the stench of your sin and death **way** over here!*

What? E-x-c-u-s-e **me?**

PHEW! I'm seated at My Father's right hand, and You're not even in the gate! But I can STILL smell the stench of your hostility against My Father way over here! Phe-ww!

*Your final destination is **NOT** here. Depart from Me!*

*You who lived in opposition against The Truth of My Father's Word. Depart into outer darkness into **your** father's kingdom! For he is the father of lies, and it is h-e who is expecting you! I AM God's Word—the defender of My Father's Throne! And You pose a top-security breach!*

WHAT?

I command all gates of heaven into lockdown mode!

A contaminated one—STILL unwashed—corrupted by Satan, My Father's Enemy—pleads at the main gate.

DENY ACCESS!

I repeat!

NO ACCESS into My Father's Kingdom, since willfully unwashed, and still in the rebellion!

Full rejection!

Conversation TERMINATED!

W-w-wAIT! PLEASE! Please! Allow me to speak with Your Father for just **ONE** minute. Please!

PLEADER'S REQUEST DENIED!

DENIED?

Oh God! What did I do to be treated this way?

Unwashed?

Hostility AGAINST Your Father's Throne?

But, Your Father and I are **friends!** And I thought this is **HIS** House!

No ONE is a friend of My Father's who opposes Me!

But Your Father and I were on <u>regular</u> speaking terms! And I figured since this is H-I-S House, HE'S the One who makes the final decisions UP here! **So, WHOSE in charge?**

*For Security—I AM! And for new births and arrivals—I AM! I **ALSO** handle Creation by Word!*

CRE-A-TION? YOU? B-u-t? You were **SO** minimized on earth! Viewed as fairly insignificant by many, and completely dismissed by others.

So, p-le-ease tell me You're not a Big Deal Up here! **You just <u>have</u> to be a mere option!** A "one-of-many" choice in humanity's "god-variety package!" That's what I was told, and I believed it.

And—like Eve—you were deceived!!!

Deceived?

No! I've always believed that You're kinda like the big guy at Christmas.

Nice to have around, but more of an add-on accessory for those who could never quite handle "the truth!"

PLEASE *let me IN!!!*

*An **add-on** accessory?*

Sure! Haven't **You** noticed? Folks are leaving You left and right! Your ratings on the earth are on the decline. And the "choose-your-own-path" to God business is a rapidly growing industry!

And I was led to believe that You are only <u>one</u> of many paths!

And—you were ALSO led to believe that there are a VARIETY of Truths!

*But, that's the deceiver's lie—because it is **h-e** who can't handle THE TRUTH!*

Oh, No. Sir, that's NO lie. There re-a-lly ARE multiple paths to God...and each individual holds their own "personal "God-path" truth"—about God!

It's both some of the highly reputable, and smome common amonng humanity who support this thought process on earth! And they can't **A-L-L** be telling... lies!

*Many—like Adam, follow unaware of where the "new path, by an old rebellion" leads—but—**LIES!!!***

Rebellion? Wait just an "earth" minute! Just who do You think You are? Lies? The truth they speak is THEIR truth—and one's personal truth is NOT to be judged—EVER! That's the rule of the EARTH down there!

Well—here's the Rule UP HERE!

I AM THE WAY, THE TRUTH AND THE LIFE and NO ONE COMES TO THE FATHER BUT BY ME!

John 14:6

Any voice that says that anyone can come to the Father, and bypass Me does not speak MY Truth! And there are some who if it were possible, would deceive even the very elect!*

*For there shall arise false Christs, and false prophets, and shall shew great signs and wonders; insomuch that, if it were possible, they shall deceive the very elect. Matthew 24:24

LXXXIV

But what about <u>MY</u> truth! Doesn't **MY** truth matter at all?

*Just who do you think **you** are? Your presence is eternally not welcomed in My Father's House!*

I'm not welcomed!?

No, **Wait!** Can we just start over? We got off to a <u>really</u> bad start!

Maybe this will help! Once, I was **somewhat** thinking about moving **You** into my life before I committed to "the flexible god" plan! It was SUCH a big decision. So I'd appreciate it if You'd TRY to understand! Really...I just **never** figured out how You could fit **comfortably** into my life!

(Pause) Yes—I was **ashamed!**

*...And for those who are **ashamed** of Me on earth, I will be ashamed of you before My Father in heaven!*

Well...wait! Once I **al-mo-o-ost** came on board with You.

__Almost__ persuaded?

To be <u>ALMOST</u> persuaded is to be ETERNALLY LOST!

Acts 26:28

[Peers with disdain and mutters] **That's ridiculous!**

AWAY into Eternal death and destruction, oh rejected one who carries earth's confusion in your heart! And who mishandled My Highly Exalted Name!

Earth's confusion? HIGHLY EXALTED? Is there **a <u>Big Deal</u>** about Your **NAME** Up here, TOO??

At the mention of My Name, <u>every</u> knee shall bow and <u>every</u> tongue confess that I Am Lord to the Glory of My Father.*

EVERY...? But what happened to make Your Name THAT **g-r-eat?**

I humbled Myself to the Cross. And through the Power of My Father's Word, I defeated death. Those who humble themselves before My Father, He exalts.* And for that reason there's over-coming Power against the work and power of the enemy, by the authority of My Name.*

But what if I <u>don't</u> *WANT to humble myself—to bow down to You,* **or** *to Your Name?*

ALL will bow—either willingly or unwillingly—maybe not in time, on the earth—where humanity holds dominion, and thus its will prevails, but in eternity—where the Will of My Father rules, and His Word is highly exalted!

So just ex-actly when does humanity's will rule, and it's word prevail in Your Father's House?

When it agrees with My Father's Will and My Father's Word— or, NOT at all! **One God! One Word! One Lord! That's exactly how it is UP Here!**

WHY I NEVER!!!

And, you never will—rule or reign with ME! For those whose will and word willfully remain in The Rebellion—are rebels who must...

Depart!

Into the darkness where rebellion rules and reigns.

Excuse me?

Again, I say "Depart!!!" Thou who has inherited **the eternal absence of My light—My Word—depart into outer darkness!

**Thy word is a lamp unto my feet, and a light unto my path. Psalm 119:105

Hungry and thirsty one!

Who rejected My eternal invitation to My feast!

VACATE THE AREA—for the Dining Room will open for serving soon!

[An attempt is made to lean into the Gate to get just a whiff of the savory meal being prepared.]

LEAVE!

But W-w-wAIT! **Food?** I NEVER intended to reject Your ***feast!***

PLEASE! What time does it start? I'm STARVIN' out here!

*Endnotes

LXXXV

TOO LATE!

*You bear not the Image of My Father, and therefore, you __cannot__ dine! This Feast is reserved ONLY for those who accepted My "Family Invitation" and are **now** the Father's children.*

But I'm SO hungry! And I thirst!

*I thirsted for you on the Cross that you despised! It is **I** Who purchased Your invitation to the Father's table.*

I came.

As God's Word!

As God!

You refused!

[Startled] Re-eally, God? **Wait.** So You and Your Father **really** are One? You really WERE

God in the Flesh on EARTH.

Yes! I CAME!

I Lived for humanity's righteousness,

I Died for humanity's forgiveness,

I ROSE for humanity's deliverance,

I ASCENDED for humanity's promise,

*and I **WILL** COME AGAIN*

for the Family's Permanent Relocation!*

*In my Father's house are many mansions: if it were not so, I would have told you. I go to prepare a place for you. And if I go and prepare a place for you, I will come again, and receive you unto myself; that where I am, there ye may be also. John 14: 2,3

LXXXVI

*I, and My Father—ARE **ONE***

But you practiced the Deceiver's math!

You "reduced" Who I AM to only—"a son"

"added" another god—or gods

*to Soverign GOD's Community of **"ONE"***

"divided" Me—the Son—from the Father

"subtracted" My Eternal Deity

"eliminated" the need for your Eternal Cleansing

and "Isolated" yourself from the Truth of God's Word,

which "carried" you over into eternal deception...

... "Eternally erring" mathmetician,

Depart!

you who "added" the Father—

*but "**SUBTRACTED**" the Son!!!*

attempting Our "division"

and "failed" to correct the error

of your eternal math equation

on earth—the "God/god" correction math lab!

***DEPART** into "subtracted" consequence*

for that is the liar's "added" portion!

*for ALL who "**subtract**" WHO I AM*

to a lesser value

than the Eternal Word of God

*will arrive at "**the liar's** sum total"*

which is death squared!

A liar??? I AM NOT A LIAR!!!

THAT IS A LIE! You LIED ABOUT ME!

"Subtracter" of the EMPTY TOMB!

And now "eternally subtracted!"

The value of your eternal

"SUM TOTAL...?"

NULL and Void...

...FULLY EMPTY

An "Eternal 0"

And now it's time to

TURN IN YOUR EarthWORK!!!

LXXXVII

But who collects my earthwork?

Where do **I turn in** it in?

And how much is a "0" WORTH

In Eternity?

Subtracted? **FULLY** EMPTY?

May I **re-do** my math?

God **please!** I want to RE-DO

my "earth math" for a better grade!

I need to **subtract** the rejection of the Son—who now **subtracts** me!

I had NO idea I'd be **graded**

on the Cross and not the curve!

I <u>cannot</u> be eternally subtracted!

What will be "added" if I'm "REDUCED" to "0" upon my final breath?

(Terrified) I hear **agonizing** screams!

LXXXVIII

[A cry from the bottom]—**HELLP ME!!! HUMANITY'S RESCUING SAVIOR! I BOW TO YOU NOW!!!! I CONFESS YOU ARE SOVEREIGN LORD AND KING!**

What's that?

It's the cry of the lost! It's the "too late" cry of eternal anguish!

Pleadings? SCREAMS? NO! I CAN'T GO! I WON'T GO!

REJECTION!

NO-O-O!!! I reject eternal rejection!

You reject? "Eternal 0," your word—your will—has no power here!

Have MERCY God, Please!

Too late!

It was MERCY'S SACRIFICE

*That you **refused**!!!!*

LXXXIX

[With humble quietness, and respect]

Please, Sir—God's Eternal Word who became Flesh,

Humanity's Savior, who is now my rejecting Judge.

Will you allow me just **one** moment to speak with You, up close?

May I come in and sit down? I am **SO** weary. I have had no rest since my arrival into eternity!

I've been searching to find a place to sit down outside of Your Father's House. And there is **no** place for me.

Please. I think I know what I can do to clear this up!

I'd like to receive You as My Savior **now***!*

Eternal Procrastinator! Are you for real?

TOO LATE!

*Rejecter of My eternal invitation! ALL Our chairs are INSIDE the Gate, and have been set up based on My pre-reserved seating list. Your name was **never** added, so you cannot remain here! Your "choosing" time has passed! And there's no provision for you.*

*The space granted for your repentance—on earth—has ended! You have arrived in eternity, on schedule, **but completely unprepared!** Nontheless, your "final-checkin" appointment still MUST still be kept!**

*For it is appointed once for a man to die, and after death the judgement! Hebrews 9:27

[Heaven's Main-Frame Computer begins to speak in a syncopated Automated Voice.]

FINAL DECISION!

ETERNAL DESTINATON SET!!!

SEAT REQUEST—DENIED!

CARELESS FREE-WILL CHOICE DECISION free-will choice decision, decision, decision! CARELE…

STOP!!

JUST LET ME DELETE IT!

I WANT TO DELETE MY **C-A-R-E-LESS** ETERNAL DECISION!

[Quietly sobbing] Please let me delete my decision.

Was I wrong? Completely **wrong?**

I want to start over!

May I start over—please!!!

Restart failure! ***"Deletion" denied due to an eternal spin!***

[God's Son speaks piercing, loudly.]

NONE BUT THE RIGHTEOUS ALLOWED BEYOND THIS POINT!!!

The Righteous? Who are they?

*Those in **right** standing with My Father—through His Son!*

(Desperate) If You're **God's Son**—then please HELP **m-e!**

XC

I did.

I was tortured!

I took you pain.

I paid Your DEATH-debt in FULL.

You refused!!! NOW—

You're DEAD to Me!

XCI

You need to leave!

The feast is scheduled to start momentarily! You are in My Way. And you are wasting My Time.

My Eternal Schedule will not be delayed. And now, My Awaited Presence is needed in the Dining Hall!

You have no reservation! Your garments are filthy, and your name is missing in the Lamb's Book of Life.!

DEPART FROM THE GATE!

But, I can get dressed **now!** If you have some extra eternal wear! I'd be glad to change. I…

…Silence! I have nothing in your "empty-life" size! You refused the invitation to My feast. You are filled with eternal deception! You have already eaten from the table of the father of emptiness and lies. So My meat and drink will not fill you.

You drank deeply from the well of eternal poison, and now you will eternally thirst!

Rejecter *of the Living Water of Life—step aside!*

You are **Living** WATER? PLEASE! **JUST ONE SIP!** P-l-ease?

As the Living Water (God) I THIRSTED for you (Man)—BUT you wanted N-O-T-H-I-N-G to do with My Provision!

Conversation...

TERMINATED!

You are eternally dismissed into Your Christ-less eternity.

XCII

Christ-less? NO GOD? Only **god!**

Completely VOID?

Please WAIT!

I BEG—as a **misinformed** PLEADER!!!!

Don't **Disconnect** from me for ETERNITY!

I don't want a false god—**the fallen god!**

I WANT THE SOVEREIGN GOD to take my soul…

FOR THE LAST TIME! MO-O-VE IT!!!

XCIII

[Dazed] Where am I now?

You are at the time of eternal reflection!

This is the place where the eternally sorrowful realize the error of having rejected humanity's Savior. And your time of eternal regret starts here.

Since you're not eligible for My, "I will never leave you nor forsake you"* promise, you will be left alone. And although feeling alone, you will have no eternal privacy! Because unlike Me, he does not knock before entering.

*For he hath said, I will never leave thee, nor forsake thee. Hebrews 13:5

Behold, I stand at the door, and knock: if any man hear my voice, and open the door, I will come in to him, and will sup with him, and he with me. Revelation 3:20

[The Dying Unbeliever types quietly and slowly while staring blankly into space. God the Father quietly unplugged upon the entrance of His Son, who refused this "new arrival's" entrance. As a result of unplugging, God is no longer available to correspond via email. Since having tuned-out, God the Son no longer speaks, and the Dying Unbeliever faces the disturbance of being eternally separated from God.]

Dear God,

Now, I can kinda see Your point. I don't recall having ever been "cleaned-up" by my god! And I guess that would mean I still need a bath. I was so "humanly" arrogant, so "self-covered" with my **"fig leaf** of personal choice," so self-assured. Did I really completely blow it? I was cocky when You and I last spoke. But I've had a rude awakening that Your Son is definitely no longer a "Sacrificial Lamb"! He has an **AT-TI-TUDE!!! And acts like He hates Me!** Being in a different family must be super offensive to Him!

AND, I had **no** idea that my entrance into eternity would end the reign of my human authority—and the influence of my human will. **Cut off!**

But God, please know I did try! I subscribed to **www. alternativepaths.com***—an eternal path agency that bypasses Your Son, but promises immediate entry into heaven. It's a site that came highly recommended! But now, I realize the site's tech team apparently doesn't know about the problems people will encounter with Your Son when using the site!!!

I've tried several times, unsuccessfully, to contact the tech department to suggest that they disable their website until something can be done to keep other users from running into the same "after-life" problem I've encountered. But

I keep getting a signal that reads, "dead response." I hope they'll read your "life-instructions" manual more thoroughly than I did.

*__www.alternativepaths.com__ is a fictitious website.

XCIV

[The Dying Unbeliever goes to a large window and views the earth, which triggers a flashback to earth's building security systems. Parallel to heaven's policy of protected, secured entrance, unauthorized entries are blocked.

Observing an office skyscraper in a large city where each person gains entry only by providing an authorizing identification—the Dying Unbeliever is deeply distraught, since being locked out of God's House.

A person who tries to pass through the security check, but does not have the necessary ID is first stopped, questioned, and is then turned away.]

Now God, I see.

Now I understand!

If major corporations on earth follow security protocols that won't allow for just **anyone** to gain access—why did I think You'd allow guaranteed access to ANYONE and EVERYONE into Your Secured Facility?

And why didn't I do the math? Your enemy who opposed Your Word got forced out due to your Justice. So why did I think those who **also** oppose Your Word would be welcomed in to live with You? Especially after Your opposer tried to bring You down, God! You don't want his opposition up there with you, again. Now, I see it so clearly. EVERY leader of a great nation has security to guard it's gates and its people—to keep its enemies out. God, You are the King, so why did I think any less of You?

XCV

[While walking aimlessly with NO direction, through blinded, tearful eyes, the Dying Unbeliever glances back at a sign in the distance, which has been posted on the main gate of heaven, and reads quietly and slowly:]

Three Bear Witness in Heaven: The Father, His Word, and the Holy Spirit: and these Three are One!

[And written beneath in blood are these exact words:]

Come clean, or stay away dirty! "Father, I gave cleansing blood!"

Note: This sign was nailed with Nail-Scarred Hands!

XCVI

[The Dying Unbeliever is jolted out of the space of eternal reflection, and meets eternal reality, hearing the booming Voice of God's Word.]

Depart from the Gate!

NO LOITERING ALLOWED!

You cannot remain here!

GO TO YOUR HOME!

Remove Yourself from My Father's Property, NOW.

(Blank stare)

Get out! You are an offense to My Father's Throne.

Eternally Unwashed One!

DEPART!

Vacate the Premisis!

NOW!!!

XCVII

❧

[God's Son types final notes into the latest E-Pad, His Eternal Electronic Device.]

Final Status:

Eternal Separation

Final Destination:

Eternally Lost

God/god Selection:

false god/fallen god

Rejecter of the Sovereign God

Attempted to "Divide God"

Attempt to embrace the Father, but refuse His Word: Denied

Name Written in the Lamb's Book of Life

No

Adam's Stain

Not Removed: active carrier of rebellion, sin, and death

Eternal Family Relationship

father - the great deceiver

Garments of Righteousness

Refused—Naked and ashamed!

Death Catagory

X First Death (Physical)

X SECOND DEATH (Spiritual)

X BOTH APPLY

Eternal Notes for Permanent Record:

When time was given to seek Me, an alternative god was willfully chosen and received. Flunked "eternal-life" math.

Refused to take My blood bath, and is now stinking up the place! (PHEW!!!)

Access to the Father's House

DENIED BY HUMANITY'S JUDGE*

For the Lord is our judge, the Lord is our lawgiver, the Lord is our king; he will save us. Isaiah 33:22

*Many will say to me in that day, Lord, Lord...And then will I profess unto them, I never knew you: depart from me, ye that work iniquity. Matthew 7:22, 23

XCVIII

Father, the Dying Unbeliever's time is out!

SON, So close, but yet SO—

XCIX

[Far away! Disturbing Sounds from *the Bottom!*]

Ha, Ha, Ha, Ha, Ha! Believer in my lies! Come NOW unto me. I am the ETERNAL DEBT COLLECTOR!!

(Laughing Recklessly) You'll be quarantined in my "hide-out, due to heaven's "social-distancing" requirements!!!

[The Dying Unbeliever falls FORCEFULLY into the hands of the waiting deceiv-v-ver, and fights DESPERATELY to be released from his gripping power! With greater strength, the enemy pushes the Dying Unbeliever into a small prison cell filled with the stench of death, filth, and the unpleasant "death oders" of the "also-dececeived" unrepentant. The Dying Unbeliever looks into the face of The Liar for the first time, and lets out an "uncleansed blood-curdling" scream. The deceiver's scratchy, anxious voice starts out slowly.]

There's an Eternal Debt that you owe—AND IT'S TO <u>M-E-e-e-e-e</u> YOU WILL PAY!

I OWE NOTHING!!! (Lie)

MY DEBT WAS PAID BY GOD'S ETERNAL SON!!! (truth)

[The reference to the Cross **infuriates** the Deceiver, causing him to stomp wildly.]

B-U-T YOU REFU-U-U-SED HIS PAYMENT— STOOPID UNBELIEVER!!! The Payment of Your Debt will start—NOW! NOW!!! And unwashed, filthy SINNER—You will pay IN FULL!!!!!

PAY UP!

YOU MUST PAY UP!

P-A-Y YOUR P-E-N-A-L-T-Y!

TO ME-e-e-e-e!

[Laughing Insanely—Recklessly!]

YOU'RE MY "**D-e-C-e-i-V-e-D**" UNBELIEVER!

[Enters another number on his "counting wall."]

Welcome HOME!

You will find my accommodations to be intensely warm with increasing heat.......

(Dead hoarsness) BUT I DON'T WANT YOU FOR MY god-d-d-d-d!!!!

N

O

O

O

O

O

O

O

O

O

O

O

O

O

O

(fades into an Eternal SCREAM!!!)

C

~~~~~

Dying Unbeliever! You're screaming! Wake up!

(Dripping with sweat) Oh, Dear God!

Was I dreaming?

It's not over? I'm not an outcast in Your Kingdom?

I **haven't** been eternally rejected?

I can **s-t-ill** gain eternal life—**through Your Son?**

*No, Dying Unbeliever! I mean, YES, Dyi-ver! Your life's not over, and You **CAN** have eternal life!!! OF COURSE! [Hilariously laughing!] But there's so little time! And you **must** accept My Son!*

Oh, God! I **d-o** want to accept Your Son! **N-o-w!** PLEASE!

I'm **S-O** glad I finally got it!

Dear God,

I Un-der-stand!

I must **NOT** reject Your Son, because I don't want Him to **reject** me!

So, was that experience **real?**

Dreaming Unbeliever,

You were dreaming. But, NOW you are…

[Both God and the Dying Unbeliever type at the same time…]

Awake!

AWAKE!

*…and you must be bathed, and get dressed in the robe of My Son's righteousness—because your garment of sin is filthy—so **deeply** stained!*

Dear God,

Do I **stink?**

(Responds through a "sin-mask.") Well, time is passing, quickly!

CI

Dying Unbeliever,

Your bath is prepared.

What kind of bath is this, God? This cleansing agent is so CLEAN—and it's Red—like crimson! OH, it's the Blood of Your Son? The Precious Blood of Your Son that washes white, as snow!

Yes!

Dear God,

What is His Name? Your Son's Name that's **highly** exalted above EVERY Name?

His Name is Jesus, the Christ, the Son of the Living God!

He IS Lord of Lords!

Emmanuel. God who came to redeem, and who now Reigns as King of Kings!

Lord Above ALL!

Oh God,

May I speak to Him?

He's listening now. He can hear you. He is near!

Jesus, please come into My heart! I am a sinner in need of Your mercy and grace!

I was separated from God through Adam's sin, and have lived separated from You because of **my own** rebellion.

Despite Your compassionate love toward me, I rejected You, so I humbly seek Your forgiveness! I ask You to forgive me, please! I was **S-O** wrong about You. Wash me with your life-cleaning blood.

I want to be God's "forever" child, so, I receive You as my Lord, my Savior. You are my *Risen King!*

(New vision) Ohhhh—God!

Who is That?

What **majestic** beauty!

What great honor! Such dignity!

His face shines like the brightness of the SUN!

And He's Crowned with a Royal Diadem!!!

That's MY Living Word!

The WORD of God—Who spoke Creation into existence!

My WORD—Creator of EARTH'S Sun!

CREATOR of Light and Life!

He IS the Radiant L-I-G-H-T of MY Truth!

Who Wears the Jeweled Diadem in Honor of His Sovereignty in Me!!!

And He is angry with me, no more!!!

CII

Who is this King of Glory?

The Lord God Almighty!

[*Bowing*] Oh God, I cannot stand in His presence.

I **must** bow down—to Him to whom every knee will bow, and every tongue confess that He IS Lord!

I **will** bow down in His presence—His triumphal presence! For His loving nearness comforts me⁓

My redeemed one!

Come unto Me,

you who have been weary and heavy laden. For I will give you rest!

[Still bowed down, now with lifted hands in adoration] The long flowing robe of Your righteous priesthood reveals that You are…

(Joins the worshiping angels) Holy, Holy, Holy!

Lord, God Almighty!

You, Who Was and Is and Is to come.

You are My Lord. My God! My Eternal King!

*[The Son Speaks in a Deep, melodious voice] And for **all** eternity to honor My Father! honor's Me—His Eternal Word!*

[Noticing] Your Voice is like the sound of living water!

So flowing, powerful and strong, yet so comforting and near.

[God the Father and the Son Speak together] **Welcome HOME!**

CIII

[Jesus speaks again, taking the Transformed Believer by the hand, while the New Believer rises to stand, gaining strength.]

Welcome to My Father, you who have come to Him through His Beloved Son, The Word.

*Through My cleansing blood, and by the work of **our** Father's Spirit, **you are connected!** Welcome, wonderfully newborn! Welcome to new life!*

Thank You!

You have removed my deep offense!

And I've been released from the power of ***our*** enemy,

the enemy of **(spoken in one voice)** "our Father."

You have completed Your work in Me,

and I—now—worship…You in Spirit and in Truth!

Well done, My good and faithful servant!

I honor You, My Majestic King.

CIV

But Your Names?

I must know Your *other* Names?

My Name is Wonderful

Counsellor

The Mighty God

The Everlasting Father

The Prince of Peace

Upon the Throne of David, I Am the Eternal Heir!

And of the increase of My Government there shall be no end!

In My Father's Kingdom flows My righteousness.

And because of the Power My Father has given unto Me—

From Everlasting to Everlasting

I Shall Eternally Reign.

CV

[Music plays softly in the background.]

Take My Hand, "Purchased" Believer! Hold My nail-scarred Hand.

They are so beautifully nail-scarred! King Jesus, May I do a dance of worship unto You?

*"Heart-Changed" Believer—I **love** a dance of worship and praise from My Family who gives back to Me!*

[The New Believer gives worshipful expression to the King. While dancing, the two speak back and forth with the worship movements nicely accompanying each word.]

Radiant Redeemer! I trust You with my life.

(Seeing the Lamb at a glance) Lamb of God. Jesus the Christ! The Redeemer of Mankind—You are the Holy Lamb, and I adore You!

I welcome you into My Father's House!

Your mansion is prepared.

Enter thou into the Joy of the Lord!

And you wear your new scent so well!

You look very lovely…so beautifully set FREE!!

CVI

[Noticing and pleasantly surprised] Oh! My tattered clothes are gone!!! My stained garments are washed, whiter than snow! Savior! I've lost my guilty stain!

So, I will clothe You in a new robe! [Jesus places a beautiful white robe on the Believer.]

Oh, My Savior! What did You place on me?

My child, it is the robe of My righteousness that has been dipped in My blood—as the perfect Sacrificial Lamb, Purely sacrificed at the Cross of Calvary!

My Father's child, Come! [In fresh "new-birth" relationship, the two walk hand in hand.]

Eldest Brother, what is that chorus that I hear? Angels voices?

No! It is the song of the redeemed!

Then, I will sing along!

"Just as I am, without one plea

But that Thy blood was shed for me

And that Thou bid'st me come to Thee

O Lamb of God, I come! I come…"

[Unexpectedly glances into the eyes of Jesus.]

Your eyes! They are like a Flame of Fire that consumes **A-L-L** unrighteousness. Is there Flaming Power in Your eyes?

Yes, "Fire-Purified" Believer. As there is Flaming Power in My Blood! To Purify My children! My child, My Father's Power flows through Me!

My LORD, and My God!

Source of life's strength.

Strength of my life!

It is in You that I live, move, and have My being.

Acts 17:28

I am eternally changed!

[Sings along, again with the chorus of the redeemed.]

A change, a change has come over me.

He changed My life, and now I'm free!

He changed my life complete.

And now I sit at His feet...

A wonderful change has come over me!

Lyrics of "Changed" by Walter Hawkins and Performed by Tramaine Hawkins (1975)

CVII

[The New Believer twirls and moves with new freedom and delight.]

Dear Father,

You wouldn't believe what just happened to me!

My child! Believing is your department!

Now, was **that** re-a-lly real, or was it a dream?

*My Child! It was **both!***

[Over the loudspeaker] Staff! Code Blue! Room 316!

Dear Heavenly Pops,

Oh, ple-ase excuse me…so sorry! I mean Heavenly "Papa."

I am **sooooooo** glad to be out of that hospital "prison" ward, and up here with You! The food they had me eating in that "'tasteless-food' contraption" was totally **yuck!** And that **tas-tel-e-s-s** water with a dead fly floatin'—almost **killed me!**

My Child, don't be too hard on them, they did their best!

[Chuckling loudly] Best! BEST! Hospital guest! I was in that **stuffy** room WAAAY too long, and could **b-a-r-ely** breathe!

Heavenly Daddy, I'm **s-o** GLAD I ESCAPED! The food is **W-A-Y** better up here! Talk about BLAND!

Yucky, puckey, shucky ducky!!! **And** "DRY" BLAND!

In fact, Heavenly Papa,

Do You think You can arrange for me to send a couple of the angels down to give that head cook some cooking lessons?

Along with that lazy one who was **skimp-y** on the Jell-O. I couldn't figure out WHY-Y-Y I couldn't get well!

Now I think it had something to do with all that **LOUSY** cookin'! A-n-d not enough crushed ice!

(Complaining fondly) And the doctor!

He didn't even get my Code correct! He said Code Blue, but it's Code Red, Daddy…

'Cuz I am **Blood** Washed!

Daddy! He was talkin' about *the* "ole' stuff!"

And speaking about blood! That nurse who hooked me to the I-V must've specialized in "patient torture!" IN FACT! She was probably workin' for Big "Mama Grande—AKA, THE MAMA!!!" (LOL)

The wrong vein punctured——twice?

OR—she was just tryin' to get back at me for almost breaking that HARD hospital bed—during **her** shift! (**"thud"** episode dra-ma!!!) (LOL, again!)

Dear God,

In case You don't know… LOL means "Laughing Out Loud" in text typing!

CVIII

My child, shhhhhhh! Welcome Home!

Oh Heavenly Daddy! I'm talking too much, aren't I? Heaven is so WONDERFUL, and I am *very* grateful to be here! I'm SO glad you stuck with me!

And btw (Remember, God?... by the way,)

[Excitedly typing] Thank You for allowing U-Turns!

[God's newest child starts making car noises and holds an invisible steering wheel, to mimic driving a fast car, and then blurts out "SCRE-E-ECH" before stopping.

The excited "baby" believer then resumes recklessly while "driving" the imaginary car—and makes a U-Turn in the middle of one of the busy streets of gold.]

My Child! Wa-ait! Watch out for speeding chariots!

Those young angels drive **FAST!**

*And bouncin' around like that, you're gonna knock over your crown! [God dives, catching the little crown that flies off, heading to the floor—just in time.]. You almost **broke it!***

(Deep exhale) Oh, well! My new born believer made it home! [God beckons Archangel Michael to come speak to Him. The Archangel leans over to hear what God whispers.]

"Arch Mike, make sure to have a Special Host of Angels stand guard over My Child until further notice! For at LEAST the first 500 years!"

"10-4" CHIEF!

[Curious Angels beckon to a couple of their cohort colleagues!] Come here quick! The Dying Unbeliever converted, and is NOW UP here with **us***!*

I don't think Heaven will **EVER** be quite the same!

OMG! SIMPLY AMAZING! Getting here was SO worth it!

This is wa-a-a-a-y Beyond SUPER COOL!

Dear Heavenly Dad,

May I call You "Heavy D" for short?

My Child—NO-PE!

Dear Heavenly D (G-LOL!)

[Giggling and laughing out loud]

My Child,

QDF (Quiet Down and FOCUS!)

Before—

CIX

[Interrupting] Dear Daddy,

Just one last question. Will I ever get a chance to meet original papa and mama?

Sure! There's Adam and Eve right over there—walking in the Garden!

[Runs to meet them.] Hello Mr. Adam and Mrs. Eve—I've been looking forward to meeting you! I'm one of your "universal children," and was recently "spirit-life" connected to our Father through Second Adam.

"We're very glad to make your acquaintance. We came to everlasting life through Him, too.

In fact, now when someone wants to tease us, they call us the Second Adam-sons.

And by the way, the Garden up Here is *wonderful.*"

Totally Coolio! Do you recommend any particular tree?

"Yes! 'The tree of life!' Just *amazing* fruit!"

Tree of life? Oh, there's some **amazing grapes**—so, I'm about to dine! And I must say it DOES feel great to be ALIVE!

[Types quickly the final "close-out" words of the email in order to make a parting request before "the original two" leave.]

Willfully,

God's Child—by Choice!

The "New-Born" Believer

P.S. In Daddy's "Forever Family!"

(Anxiously select's "print only last page" and excitedly yanks the closing page out of the printer.)

"Excuse me, please. But, do you two mind signing your names right there?"

"We'd be honored!"

"Eternally Risen in Christ!"

Adam and Eve

[Adam and Eve join the Second Adam as He passes by. The Newest Unbeliever joins the party, only to learn that they are all headed to the Banquet Hall for a scrumptious "Invitation Only" Family Feast.]

Glancing back and gesturing to the World,
God's Son graciously inquires...

"Living water anyone?"

"I will come again, and receive you unto myself;
that where I am, there ye may be also."
John 14:3

And when you are converted, be baptized, (as an outward expression of your inward washing and change!) Acts 2:38

"Jesus is coming soon! Are you ready to meet Him?"

In Memory of My Darling Mother, Oracia (her name means "Oracle of God".) Mama placed God's Living Word deeply in my heart, and seized every opportunity to share the love of Jesus with those who passed her way. It is to my mother that, I dedicate *Last Minute Emails to God from a Dying Unbeliever: Dear God, Which Way Is UP?*

Now with the Lord, she served her Savior, her family, and her generation with her **whole** heart! And now, I advance the torch of faith that she passed to me for the cause of the gospel of Christ! Each of her children serve in Christian ministry.

In Loving Memory of Cousin Olivia—My cousin Ted's mother who loved the Lord, deeply. Ted—what your mother told you in her departure was a great treasure. Meet your mom there—she's now at home with Jesus.

I also dedicate *Emails to God from a Dying Unbeliever* to my dad, Reverend Luther, a *Mighty Warrior* in God's Army! Thanks, Dad, for your incredible help with this project! You are not only a church and business founder, but you were a great husband of 55 years, and are an awesome father. Last but not least, you are also quite an editor! At 87, you're still on the cutting-edge—sharp, alert, and witty! I love you dad! As the *"Bumble-Bee,"* who has *always* defied the limits of your wings, you still are in flight.

A Tribute to Edith's daughter, Sabreem

To those of us who loved her, Sabreem went home to heaven way too early, it seems. But out of her passing came a dedicated mother's commitment to sponsor *Dear God, Which Way is Up?* As a tribute to her beautiful daughter, with great generosity, Edith, my *dear* friend, made it possible for me to meet the requirements to publish with TBN!

Out of Sabreem's homegoing, many souls will be won for the kingdom of God! For as the many Dying Unbelievers evangelized by this book enter into heaven, I believe God will allow Edith's daughter, who found faith at an early age, to help welcome them in with her big, beaming smile!

Edith, I thank you, and your family—Marvin, Omar and Kaseem. You are a very dear sister and friend!

I also dedicate this book to the dying unbelievers everywhere who will accept Jesus Christ as their Lord and Savior while reading this inspired message of hope.

Acknowledgements

Edith ~ You are a dear friend—always ready with a laugh, a prayer, and a word of encouragement. Your kind generosity made this book launch! Kudos!

To Dr. Deborah M. ~ What a gifted author you are! I was grateful when you joined the writing project, and disappointed when you had to leave so shortly afterwards. And despite changing the book's direction after your departure, I'll always hold fond memories of our "café writing" experiences! For the times your feedback has sharpened an area of my work—a huge thanks! P.S. Still waiting for your hourly rate (smiles).

To My brother, Mike, and Dr. LaTonya D.~ Dr. D, your feedback that led to my idea of birthing the Dying Unbeliever set me in a good direction, and I have never looked back! Mike, your insight that I should clarify the most important question: Who does the Dying Unbeliever _not_ believe in— required that I provide increased clarification. Now, it is crystal clear! As is Invictus—the Maestro's loveliest of songs!

Diane ~ Sending love from your "lil" sis.

Sarah ~ My friend. When I started this journey, you were so gracious with encouragement. I'll always remember.

Jane ~ Thank you for the kind generosity you show to so many, as a role model of excellence. May God continue to prosper you.

Pastor Katherine ~ In giving, you sowed, and the harvest is here! Yes, reaping is ahead.

To my colleague, Peggy ~ The day you told your son, one day he would purchase my book at Barnes and Noble, I felt so encouraged. And look! God has brought it to pass!

Mother James ~ What a prayer warrior you are! God is faithful to you, as His daughter and special friend!

Ella ~ My dear sister. Here's your long awaited "Special Edition" copy. Enjoy.

"Cousin Sam" and Lady B. ~ Thank you for sharing invaluable feedback. But God!

To my Attorney, Cindy ~ Thank you for your expertise and guidance. You are a precious jewel.

Ileene ~ Peace, blessings and God's prosperity to you and the Bishop.

Lisa ~ You are a bright light, and your love is felt in the Golden State.

Cheryl ~ From the "M" to the "T" and Beyond! God's work offers eternal benefits for His faithful employees!

Dr. Bridget ~ Thank you for your gift of courage. It motivated me to include ALL of what needed to be spoken through this writing. Thus, I finished my charge!

Lady Deborah and Pastor ~ Because of you, the "Last Mile" of a long journey was completed on Holy Ground. Peace and Blessings, always!

Mother Caldwell ~ "God put the rainbow in the sky, and love in your heart." You are a mother of mothers.

Pastor Bob ~ Three plus years ago, I shared words on a napkin with you that God transformed into this book. What a miracle!

Pastor Mitchell ~ thank you for your feedback. Insightful, indeed.

Lily ~ You are such a powerful servant leader—equipped, capable, and always ready to assist with precision. Keep up the good work.

Mark, Bryan, Misty, Kelli, and Noah TBN's TRILOGY's staff ~ What a phenomenal opportunity! Misty and Kelli—we finished…an awesome job by an awesome editorial team!

Stephen, Gabe, and Yvonne ~ I love you, family!

Frances ~ You have a heart of great giving, you will receive a great reward. Thank you for your wisdom.

To my daughter, Destani Oracia ~ There is such an *awesome* call of God on your life! Release the writing talent God has given you for *His* glory! God has His hands on you!

"Brilliant, witty, and a master of words~" That's who you are, Ramona. God sent you to walk with me and the Dying Unbeliever over the finish line. BA-AAM!

To every radio and television pastor whose word crossed my hearing just in time to clarify an idea I pondered about God's truth. God speed for your faithful service!

And to the Hillsong pastor's wife ~ Your word fitly spoken…"This is a mustard seed that will grow into a great Oak Tree." Through God's grace, I planted, TBN has watered, and God will give the increase!!!

Endnotes

"Jesus saith unto him, I am the way, the truth, and the life: no man cometh unto the Father, but by me." John 14:6

Jesus said,… "I am the resurrection, and the life." John 11:25

"For there are three that bear record in heaven, the Father, the Word, and the Holy Ghost: and these three are one." I John 5:7

O death, where is thy sting? O grave, where is thy victory?
1 Corinthians 15:55-57 King James Version (KJV)

Chapter III
Now the serpent was more subtil than any beast of the field which the LORD God had made. And he said unto the woman, Yea, hath God said, Ye shall not eat of every tree of the garden? **And the woman said unto the serpent, We may eat of the fruit of the trees of the garden:** *But of the fruit of the tree which is in the midst of the garden, God hath said, Ye shall not eat of it, neither shall ye touch it, lest ye die. And the serpent said unto the woman, Ye shall not surely die: For God doth know that in the day ye eat thereof, then your eyes shall be opened, and ye shall be as gods, knowing good and evil. Genesis 3:1-5*

And when the woman saw that the tree was good for food, and that it was pleasant to the eyes, and a tree to be desired to make one wise, she took of the fruit thereof, and did eat, and gave also unto her husband with her; and he did eat. Genesis 3:6

So the LORD God took the man [He had made] and settled him in the Garden of Eden to cultivate and keep it. And the LORD God commanded the man, saying, "You may freely (unconditionally) eat [the fruit] from every tree of the garden, but [only] from the tree of the knowledge (recognition) of good and evil you shall not eat, otherwise on the day that you eat from it, you shall most certainly die [because of your disobedience]." Genesis 2:15-17 The Amplified Bible

Chapter IX
When a person makes a decision to complete a certain action, the will is in operation. A part of the soul is the will. Job 7:15 says, "My soul would choose," and 6:7 says, "My soul refuses…" To choose and to refuse are both decisions and functions of the will.! Chronicles 22:19 says, "Now set your heart and your soul to seek after Jehovah your God." We set our soul to seek and to choose the path we will take.

Chapter X
And so it is written, The first man Adam was made a living soul; the last Adam was made a quickening spirit (1 Corinthians 15:45). Note: And the Second Adam was Gods Son, who was His Word made flesh.

Know ye not, that to whom ye yield yourselves servants to obey, his servants ye are to whom ye obey; whether of sin unto death, or of obedience unto righteousness? (Romans 6:16)

Chapter XII
For the life of the flesh is in the blood. Leviticus 17:11

And He said, "What have you done? The voice of your brother's blood cries out to Me from the ground.

Genesis 4:10 New King James Version
And to Jesus the mediator of the new covenant, and to the blood of sprinkling, that speaketh better things than that of Abel. Hebrews 12:24

The fool hath said in his heart, There is no God. Psalm 14:1

"All right, you may test him," the LORD said to Satan. "Do whatever you want with everything he possesses, but don't harm him physically." So Satan left the LORD's presence. Job 1:12

But, beloved, do not forget this one thing, that with the Lord one day is as a thousand years, and a thousand years as one day.

Now Faith is the substance of things hoped for, and the evidence of things not seen. Hebrews 11:1

Without faith it is impossible to please God. Hebrews 11:6

And God said, Let us make man in our image, after our likeness: and let them have dominion over the fish of the sea, and over the fowl of the air, and over the cattle, and over all the earth. Genesis 1:26

Chapter XV
For the Lord himself shall descend from heaven with a shout, with the voice of the archangel, and with the trump of God: and the dead in Christ shall rise first: Then we which are alive and remain shall be caught up together with them in the clouds, to meet the Lord in the air: and so shall we ever be with the Lord (1 Thessalonians 4:16-17).

Chapter XXI
* *According as his divine power hath given unto us **all** things that pertain unto **life and godliness**. 2 Peter 1, 3*

You belong to your father, the devil, and you want to carry out your father's desires. He was a murderer from the beginning, not holding to the truth, for there is no truth in him. When he lies, he speaks his native language, for he is a liar and the father of lies. John 8:44 International Version

Chapter XXII
On that day his feet will stand on the Mount of Olives…The Lord will be king over the whole earth. On that day there will be one Lord, and his name the only name. Zachariah 14:4, 9 New International Version

And you *He made alive,* who…once walked according to the course of this world, **according to the prince of the power of the air.** Ephesians 2:1, 2. New King James Version

But the ship was now in the midst of the sea, tossed with waves: for the wind was contrary…And when the disciples saw him walking on the sea, they were troubled…and they cried out for fear. But straightway Jesus spake unto them, saying, Be of good cheer; it is I; be not afraid. Matthew 14:24-27

And he arose, and rebuked the wind, and said unto the sea, Peace, be still. And the wind ceased, and there was a great calm. Mark 4:39

Chapter XXV
Unto Adam also and to his wife did the LORD God make coats of skins, and clothed them. Genesis 3:21

Without the shedding of blood, there is no remission (of sin). Hebrews 9:22

Remit: To refrain from exacting a tax or penalty; to cancel.

More on the Adam and Eve story from Chapter XXV.

And Adam called his wife's name Eve; because she was the mother of all living (Genesis 3:20).

And the man said, The woman whom thou gavest to be with me, she gave me of the tree, and I did eat. Genesis 3:12

And the LORD God said to the woman, "What is this you have done?" The woman said, "The serpent deceived me, and I ate" (Genesis 3:12 NKJV).

Atonement—repair for an offense.

And the eyes of them both were opened, and they knew that they were naked; and they sewed fig leaves together, and made themselves aprons (Genesis 3:7).

Chapter XXIX
*For the Son of man is come to **seek and to save that which was lost** (Luke 19:10).*

He went once for all into the Holy Place [the Holy of Holies of heaven, into the presence of God], and not through the blood of goats and calves, but through His own blood, having obtained and secured eternal redemption [that is, the salvation of all who personally believe in Him as Savior] (Hebrews 9:12 AMP).

Note: The scripture references below are taken from Chapter XXX.

*What is man, that thou art mindful of him? or the son of man that thou visitest him? Thou madest him a little lower than the angels; thou crownedst him with glory and honour, and didst set him over the works of thy hands (Hebrews 2:6-7).

*He has made everything beautiful in its time. He has also set eternity in the hearts of men (Ecclesiastes 3:11).

The earth is the Lord's, and the fulness thereof; the world, and they that dwell therein. Psalm 24:1

Now the serpent was more subtil than any beast of the field which the Lord God had made. And he said unto the woman, Yea, hath God said, Ye shall not eat of every tree of the garden? Genesis 3:1

Chapter XXXIX

So the LORD God sent them out of the Garden of Eden, where they would have to work the ground from which the man had been made (Genesis 3:23 CEV).

Then to Adam He said, "Because you have listened to the voice of your wife, and have eaten from the tree about which I commanded you, saying, 'You shall not eat from it'; Cursed is the ground because of you; In toil you will eat of it All the days of your life (Genesis 3:17 NIV).

And if I go and prepare a place for you, I will come again, and receive you unto myself; that where I am, there ye may be also" (John 14:3).

Come unto me, all ye that labour and are heavy laden, and I will give you rest. Take my yoke upon you, and learn of me; for I am meek and lowly in heart: and ye shall find rest unto your souls. For my yoke is easy, and my burden is light (Matthew 11:28-30).

"There remaineth therefore a rest to the people of God." Hebrews 4:9

*In the beginning God created the heaven and the earth…And God **said**, Let there be light: and there was light. And God saw the light, that it was good: Genesis 1:1,3*

*Note: God **spoke** His word to create light.*

Chapter XLII
That which has been is that which will be, And that which has been done is that which will be done. So there is nothing new under the sun. Ecclesiastes 1:9

Chapter XLIII
And I will put enmity between you and the woman, and between your seed and her seed. He will crush your head, and you will strike his heel" (Genesis 3:15 BSB).

Chapter XLVII
Through faith we understand that the worlds were framed by the word of God, so that things which are seen were not made of things which do appear. Hebrews 11:3

Chapter XLIX.
For unto us a child is born, unto us a son is given… And the government shall be upon his shoulder: and his name shall be called Wonderful, Counsellor, The mighty God, The everlasting Father, The Prince of Peace. Isaiah 9:6.

Have this same attitude (mind) in yourselves which was in Christ Jesus… who, although He existed in the form and unchanging essence of God…did not regard equality with God a thing to be grasped or asserted…but emptied Himself [without renouncing or diminishing His deity…]. Phillipians 2: 5-7. AMP

*For I **came** down from heaven, not to do mine own **will**, but **the will of him that sent me**. And this is the **Father's will** which hath **sent me**, **that of** all which he hath given me I should lose nothing, but should raise it up again at the last day. John 6:38,39*

"And the devil, taking him up into an high mountain, shewed unto him all the kingdoms of the world in a moment of time. And the devil said unto him, All this power will I give thee, and the glory of them: for that is delivered unto

me; and to whomsoever I will I give it. If thou therefore wilt worship me, all shall be thine. And Jesus answered and said unto him, Get thee behind me, Satan: for it is written, Thou shalt worship the Lord thy God, and him only shalt thou serve." John 4:5-8

Chapter LV

*Jesus said unto them, Verily, verily, I say unto you, Before **Abraham was**, **I am**. Then took they up stones to cast at him: but Jesus hid himself, and went out of the temple, going through the midst of them, and so passed by. John 8: 58, 59*

Chapter LVI

And about the ninth hour Jesus cried with a loud voice, saying, 'Eli, Eli, lama sabachthani?' that is to say, "My God, my God, why hast thou forsaken me?" Matthew 27:46

Chapter LVIII

*For **You will not leave my soul in** Sheol, Nor will You allow Your Holy One to see **corruption**. Psalm 16:10*

*He will **crush** your **head**, **and** you will **bruise His heel**. Genesis 3:15*

Chapter LXXXIV

At the name of Jesus every knee should bow, of those in heaven, and of those on earth, and of those under the earth, and that every tongue should confess that Jesus Christ is Lord, to the glory of God the Father. Philippians 2:10-11 NKJV

And there's overcoming Power against the work and power of the enemy, by the authority of My Name.

*And these signs shall follow them that believe; In my **name shall they cast out** devils; they shall speak with new tongues… they shall lay hands on the sick, and they shall recover. Mark 16:17-18*

And being found in fashion as a man, he humbled himself, and became obedient unto death, even the death of the cross. Wherefore God also hath highly exalted him, and given him a name which is above every name: Philippians 2:8-9

*Whosoever shall exalt **himself shall be** humbled, and he that shall humble **himself shall** he **exalted**. Matthew 23:12*

Chapter References End Here

So also [is] the resurrection of the dead. It is sown in corruption; it is raised in incorruption. I Corinthians 14:42

And I wept much, because no man was found worthy to open and to read the book, neither to look thereon. And one of the elders saith unto me, Weep not: behold, the Lion of the tribe of Judah, the Root of David, hath prevailed to open the book, and to loose the seven seals thereof. And I beheld, and, lo…in the midst of the elders, stood a Lamb as it had been slain… Revelations 5:5,6

God blessed them and said to them, "Be fruitful and increase in number; fill the earth and subdue it. Rule over the fish in the sea and the birds in the sky and over every living creature that moves on the ground." Genesis 1:28 New International Version

But as many as received him, to them gave he power to become the children of God, even to them that believe on his name (John 1:12).

Heaven and earth shall pass away, but my words shall not pass away. Matthew 24:35 King James Version (KJV)

By which also he (Jesus) went and preached unto the spirits in prison. I Peter 3:19

"And I will put enmity between you and the woman, and between your offspring and hers; he will crush your head, and you will strike his heel." Genesis 3:15 NIV

What? know ye not that your body is the temple of the Holy Ghost which is in you… I Corinthians 6:19

If we confess our sins, he is faithful and just to forgive us our sins, and to cleanse us from all unrighteousness. 1 John 1:9 King James Version (KJV)

And God said, Let us make man in our image, after our likeness: and let them have dominion over the fish of the sea, and over the fowl of the air, and over the cattle, and over all the earth, and over every creeping thing that creepeth upon the earth. Genesis 1:26-28 King James Version (KJV)

And as it is appointed unto men once to die, but after this the judgment: Hebrews 9:27

Looking unto Jesus the author and finisher of our faith; who for the joy that was set before him endured the cross, despising the shame, and is set down at the right hand of the throne of God. Hebrews 12:2

In which you once walked according to the course of this world, according to the prince of the power of the air, the spirit who now works in the sons of disobedience, Ephesians 2:2

Great peace have they that love they law, and nothing shall offend them. Psalm 119:165

What is man, that thou art mindful of him? and the son of man, that thou visitest him? For thou hast made him a little lower than the angels, and hast crowned him with glory and honour. Thou madest him to have dominion over the works of thy hands; thou hast put all things under his feet. Psalm 8:4-6

The mandatory payment for sin is eternal death, but fallen humanity in its sinful condition could not pay this penalty. (See Romans 6:23.)

Since without the shedding of pure blood there is no removal of sin (Hebrews 9:22), the purifying payment for humanity's pardon and cleansing required a perfect sacrifice. Thus, God's Eternal Son came to humanity, offered Himself up as humanity's cleansing purifier, and in so doing became our unstained deliverer. The Son of God was heaven's eternal solution to humanity's eternal problem of death caused by sin. Second Adam is another name for God's Son, Jesus Christ (I Corinthians 15:45; 15:22).

"And there was war in heaven: Michael and his angels fought against the dragon; and the dragon fought and his angels, And prevailed not; neither was their place found any more in heaven. And the great dragon was cast out, that old serpent, called the Devil, and Satan, which deceiveth the whole world: he was cast out into the earth, and his angels were cast out with him." Revelation 12: 7-9 (Also read verses 10-12.)

[10] And I heard a loud voice saying in heaven, Now is come salvation, and strength, and the kingdom of our God, and the power of his Christ: for the accuser of our brethren is cast down, which accused them before our God day and night.
[11] And they overcame him by the blood of the Lamb, and by the word of their testimony; and they loved not their lives unto the death.

[12] Therefore rejoice, ye heavens, and ye that dwell in them. Woe to the inhabiters of the earth and of the sea! for the devil is come down unto you, having great wrath, because he knoweth that he hath but a short time.

"And hath made of one blood all nations of men for to dwell on all the face of the earth, and hath determined the times before appointed, and the bounds of their habitation." Acts 17:26

"Are not all angels ministering spirits sent to serve those who will inherit salvation?" Hebrews 1:14 (NIV)

So it is written: "The first man Adam became a living being"; the last Adam, a life-giving spirit.

"Behold, all souls are mine... the soul that sinneth, it shall die." Ezekiel 18:4

"Father, if You are willing, remove this cup from Me; yet not My will, but Yours be done." Luke 22:42 (NASB) Note: The cup that Jesus refers to is the bitter cup of sin and death. Father God did not remove it, and so Jesus drank from it. In His drinking of it, this partaking allowed Him to access Adam's sin. In His death, where He shed His pure and innocent blood, Adam, became the substitutionary sacrifice for humanity. Jesus took humankind's place on the Cross.

"Submit yourselves therefore to God. Resist the devil, and he will flee from you." James 4:7-10

"And this is why it was written: In the beginning was the Word, and the Word was with God and the Word was God. And the Word was made Flesh and dwelt among us,(and we beheld his glory, the glory as of the only begotten of the Father), full of grace and truth." John 1:1, 14

"But do not forget this one thing, dear friends: With the Lord a day is like a thousand years, and a thousand years are like a day." 2 Peter 3:8 (NIV)

"If the Son therefore shall make you free, ye shall be free indeed." John 8:36

"Unto Adam also and to his wife did the Lord God make coats of skins, and clothed them." Genesis 3:21

"For the life of the flesh is in the blood: and I have given it to you upon the altar to make an atonement for your souls: for it is the blood that maketh an atonement for the soul." Leviticus 17:11

Atonement: reparation for (the repair of) a wrong or injury.
"But we are all as an unclean *thing*, and all our righteousness *is* as filthy rags..." Isaiah 46:6

"... written in the book of life of the Lamb slain from the foundation of the world." Revelations 13:8

"And they overcame him by the blood of the Lamb, and by the word of their testimony; and they loved not their lives unto the death." Revelation 12:11

"No man can come to me, except the Father which hath sent me draw him: and I will raise him up at the last day." John 6:44

"But he was wounded for our transgressions, he was bruised for our iniquities: the chastisement of our peace was upon him; and with his stripes we are healed." Isaiah 53:5-8

"Jesus answered and said unto him, Verily, verily, I say unto thee, except a man be born again, he cannot see the kingdom of God. Jesus answered, Verily, verily, I say unto thee, except a man be born of water and of the Spirit, he cannot enter into the kingdom of God." John 3:3-6

"And the Spirit and the bride say, Come. And let him that heareth say, Come. And let him that is athirst come. And whosoever will, let him take the water of life freely." Revelation 22:17

"For whosoever shall do the will of my Father which is in heaven, the same is my brother, and sister, and mother." Matthew 12:50

"Who is the image of the invisible God, the firstborn of every creature." Colossians 1:15

"After this manner therefore pray ye: Our Father which art in heaven, Hallowed be thy name. Thy kingdom come, Thy will be done in earth, as it is in heaven." Matthew 6:9-10

"But about that day or hour (of Jesus' return) no one knows, not even the angels in heaven, nor the Son, but only the Father." Matthew 24:36

"I and my Father are one." John 10:30

"For I did not speak on My own initiative, but the Father Himself who sent Me has given Me a commandment as to what to say and what to speak." John 12:49

"And I will pray the Father, and he shall give you another Comforter, that he may abide with you forever." John 14:16

"For there are three that bear record in <u>heaven</u>, the <u>Father</u>, the Word, and the Ghost: and these three are one." I John 5:7

"I have much more to say to you, more than you can now bear. But when he, the Spirit of truth, comes, he will guide you into all the truth. He will not speak on his own; he will speak only what he hears, and he will tell you what is yet to come. He will glorify me because it is from me that he will receive what he will make known to you." John 16:12-14 (NIV)

"In whom we have redemption through his blood, even the forgiveness of sins: Who is the image of the invisible God, the firstborn of every creature." Colossians 1:14-15

"For unto us a child is born, unto us a son is given... And the government shall be upon his shoulder: and his name shall be called Wonderful, Counsellor, The mighty God, The everlasting Father, The Prince of Peace. Of the increase of his government and peace there shall be no end, upon the throne of David, and upon his kingdom, to order it, and to establish it with judgment and with justice from henceforth even forever. The zeal of the Lord of hosts will perform this." Isaiah 9:6-7

"And the angel answered and said unto her, The Holy Ghost shall come upon thee, and the power of the Highest shall overshadow thee, therefore also that holy thing which shall be born of thee shall be called the Son of God." Luke 1:35

"And He is the radiance of His glory and the exact representation of His nature, and upholds all things by the word of His power. When He had made purification of sins, He sat down at the right hand of the Majesty on high." Hebrews 1:3 (NASB)

My sheep hear my voice, and I know them, and they follow me. And I give unto them eternal life; and they shall never perish, neither shall any man pluck them out of my hand." John 10:27-28

"For even hereunto were ye called: because Christ also suffered for us... Who his own self bare our sins in his own body on the tree, that we, being dead to sins, should live unto righteousness: by whose stripes ye were healed." I Peter 2:21-24

"Leaving us an example, that ye should follow his steps: Who did no sin, neither was guile found in his mouth: Who, when he was reviled, reviled not again; when he suffered, he threatened not; but committed himself to him that judgeth righteously: Who his own self bare our sins in his own body on the tree, that we, being dead to sins, should live unto righteousness: by whose stripes ye were healed." I Peter 2:21-24

"For there shall arise false Christs, and false prophets, and shall shew great signs and wonders; insomuch that, if it were possible, they shall deceive the very elect." Matthew 24:24

"For whosoever shall be ashamed of me and of my words, of him shall the Son of man be ashamed, when he shall come in his own glory, and in his Father's, and of the holy angels." Luke 9:26.

"Almost thou persuadest me to be a Christian." Acts 26:28

"Let not your heart be troubled: ye believe in God, believe also in me. In my Father's house are many mansions: if it were not so, I would have told you. I go to prepare a place for you. And if I go and prepare a place for you, I will come again, and receive you unto myself; that where I am, there ye may be also." John 14:1-3

"The thief cometh not, but for to steal, and to kill, and to destroy: I am come that they might have life, and that they might have it more abundantly. I am the good shepherd: the good shepherd giveth his life for the sheep." John 10:10-12

"It is Christ that died, yea rather, that is risen again, who is even at the right hand of God, who also maketh intercession for us." Romans 8:34

"'Shout and be glad, Daughter Zion. For I am coming, and I will live among you, 'declares the Lord. "Many nations will be joined with the

Lord in that day and will become my people. I will live among you and you will know that the Lord Almighty has sent me to you." Zechariah 2:10-11 (NIV)

"'For I know the plans I have for you,' declares the Lord, 'plans to prosper you and not to harm you, plans to give you hope and a future.'" Jeremiah 29:11

"I am watching over My word to perform it." Jeremiah 1:12 (NASB)

"Let the redeemed of the LORD say so, whom he hath redeemed from the hand of the enemy." Psalm 107:2

"Behold, he cometh with clouds; and every eye shall see him, and they also which pierced him: and all kindreds of the earth shall wail because of him. Even so, Amen."

Revelation 1:7"Then we which are alive and remain shall be caught up together with them in the clouds, to meet the Lord in the air: and so shall we ever be with the Lord. "I Thessalonians 4:17

"For as the lightning cometh out of the east, and shineth even unto the west; so shall also the coming of the Son of man be. But of that day and hour knoweth no man, no, not the angels of heaven, but my Father only." Matthew 24:27;38

"Then you will understand what is right and just and fair—every good path. For wisdom will enter your heart, and knowledge will be pleasant to your soul." Proverbs 2:9-10 (NIV)

"A good man out of the good treasure of his heart bringeth forth that which is good; and an evil man out of the evil treasure of his heart bringeth forth that which is evil: for of the abundance of the heart his mouth speaketh." Luke 6:45

"Who *is* this King of glory? The LORD strong and mighty, the LORD mighty in battle." Psalm 24:8

"The LORD is a man of war: the LORD is his name." Exodus 15:3.

"And to Jesus the mediator of the new covenant, and to the blood of sprinkling, that speaketh better things than *that of* Abel." Hebrews 12:24

Jesus died a substitutionary death, taking the place of every member of humanity. In so doing, He paid the eternal death penalty required for Adam's sin, as inherited by Adam's family—humanity. Since stained by sin and death, fallen humanity could not offer the *perfect sacrifice* required for its purification and pardon. But through Christ, cleansing coverage is available to all who will receive. (2 Corinthians 5:21; I Peter 2:24; I Peter 3:18)

"For I came down from heaven, not to do mine own will, but the will of him that sent me." John 6:38

"God made the world and all things therein... And hath made of one blood all nations of men for to dwell on all the face of the earth..." (Acts 17: 24 and 26a). Because God gave Adam the command *not* to eat of the Forbidden Tree, it was Adam, not Eve, who was held responsible to God for obedience (Genesis 2:16-17).

"All we like sheep have gone astray; we have turned everyone to his own way; and the LORD hath laid on him the iniquity of us all. He was oppressed, and he was afflicted, yet he opened not his mouth: he is brought as a lamb to the slaughter, and as a sheep before her shearers is dumb, so he opened not his mouth. He was taken from prison and from judgment: and who shall declare his generation? for he was cut off out of the land of the living: for the transgression of my people was he stricken." Isaiah 53:5-8

"Nicodemus saith unto him, how can a man be born when he is old? can he enter the second time into his mother's womb, and be born? That which is born of the flesh is flesh; and that which is born of the Spirit is spirit." John 3:3-6

"Thy kingdom come, thy will be done in earth, as it is in heaven. Give us this day our daily bread and forgive us our debts, as we forgive our debtors, and lead us not into temptation, but deliver us from evil: For thine is the kingdom, and the power, and the glory, forever. Amen." Matthew 6:10-13

"But with the precious blood of Christ, as of a lamb without blemish and without spot: Who verily was foreordained before the foundation of the world, but was manifest in these last times for you, Who by him do believe in God, that raised him up from the dead, and gave him glory; that your faith and hope might be in God. Seeing ye have purified your souls in obeying the truth through the Spirit unto unfeigned love of the brethren, see that ye love one another with a pure heart fervently: Being born again, not of corruptible seed, but of incorruptible, by the word of God, which liveth and abideth forever. For all flesh is as grass, and all the glory of man as the flower of grass. The grass withereth, and the flower thereof falleth away: But the word of the Lord endureth forever. And this is the word which by the gospel is preached unto you." 1 Peter 1:19-25

"Who, being in the form of God, thought it not robbery to be equal with God, but made himself of no reputation, and took upon him the form of a servant, and was made in the likeness of men: And being found in fashion as a man, he humbled himself, and became obedient unto death, even the death of the cross, wherefore God also hath highly exalted him, and given him a name which is above every name. That at the name of Jesus every knee should bow, of things in heaven, and things in earth, and things under the earth, and that every tongue should confess that Jesus Christ is Lord, to the glory of God the Father, wherefore, my beloved…. work out your own salvation with fear and trembling." Philippians 2:6-12

It was Adam's sinful rebellion that resulted in the fall. Adam's introduction of sin and death into the human equation, resulted in humanity's separation from God. So, in Adam all die (spiritually and physically), but in Christ all shall all be made alive, spiritually and then physically when those who die in Christ will resurrect to new life, eternally, in a glorified body. (I Corinthians 15:22; John 11:25;John 6:39; I Corinthians 15:42-44; Luke 24:39; I John 3:2)

"He who has an ear, let him hear what the Spirit says to the churches. To him who overcomes I will give to eat from the tree of life, which is in the midst of the Paradise of God." Revelation 2:7

…the glory of Christ, who is the exact likeness of God. 2 Corinthians 4:4 New Living Translation (NLT)

And out of the ground made the Lord God to grow every tree that is pleasant to the sight, and good for food; the tree of life also in the midst of the garden, and the tree of knowledge of good and evil. Genesis 2:9

Do you not know that your bodies are temples of the Holy Spirit, who is in you, whom you have received from God? You are not your own; you were bought at a price. Therefore honor God with your bodies. 1 Corinthians 6:19-20 New International Version (NIV)

"Because you listened to your wife and ate fruit from the tree about which I commanded you, 'You must not eat from it,'

"Cursed is the ground because of you; through painful toil you will eat food from it all the days of your life. Genesis 3:17 New Language Translation

...the high priest (went) alone once every year, not without blood, which he offered for himself, and for the errors of the people: But Christ being come an high priest of good things to come, by a greater and more perfect tabernacle, not made with hands, that is to say, not of this building; Neither by the blood of goats and calves, but by his own blood he entered in once into the holy place, having obtained eternal redemption for us. For if the blood of bulls and of goats, and the ashes of an heifer sprinkling the unclean, sanctifieth to the purifying of the flesh: How much more shall the blood of Christ, who through the eternal Spirit offered himself without spot to God, purge your conscience from dead works to serve the living God? Hebrews 9:7,11-14

And God spake all these words, saying, "I am the Lord thy God, which have brought thee out of the land of Egypt, out of the house of bondage. Thou shalt have no other gods before me. Thou shalt not make unto thee any graven image, or any likeness of anything that is in heaven above, or that is in the earth beneath, or that is in the water under the earth. Thou shalt not bow down thyself to them, nor serve them: for I the Lord thy God am a jealous God, visiting the iniquity of the fathers upon the children unto the third and fourth generation of them that hate me; And shewing mercy unto thousands of them that love me, and keep my commandments." Exodus 20:1-6

But each one of us was given grace according to the measure of the gift of Christ. Therefore God says, 'When he ascended on high, he led captivity captive, and gave gifts to men.' But this, 'He ascended'—didn't he also first descend into the lower parts of the earth? He who descended is the one who also ascended far above all the heavens, that he might fill all things" Ephesians 4:7-10, quoting Psalm 68:18.

For you will not leave my soul in hell; neither will you suffer your Holy One to see corruption. Psalm 16:10, Acts 2:27

And about the ninth hour Jesus cried with a loud voice, saying, Eli, Eli, lama sabachthani? that is to say, My God, my God, why hast thou forsaken me? Matthew 27:46 King James Version (KJV)

Ye (speaking to the Pharisees) are of your father the devil… He… abode not in the truth, because there is no truth in him. When he speaketh a lie, he speaketh of his own: for he is a liar, and the father of it. John 8:44 King James Version (KJV)

Have this same attitude in yourselves which was in Christ Jesus [look to Him as your example in selfless humility], who, although He existed in the form *and* unchanging essence of God [as One with Him, possessing the fullness of all the divine attributes—the entire nature of deity], did not regard equality with God a thing to be grasped *or* asserted [as if He did not already possess it, or was afraid of losing it]; but emptied Himself [without renouncing or diminishing His deity, but only temporarily giving up the outward expression of divine equality and His rightful dignity] by assuming the form of a bond-servant, and being made in the likeness of men [He became completely human but was without sin, being fully God and fully man]. After He was found in [terms of His] outward appearance as a man [for a divinely-appointed time], He humbled Himself [still further] by becoming obedient [to the Father] to the point of death, even death on a cross. For this reason also [because He obeyed and so completely humbled Himself], God has highly exalted Him and bestowed on Him the name which is above every name, so that at the name of Jesus]every knee shall bow [in submission], of those who are in heaven and on earth and under the earth, and that every tongue will confess *and* openly acknowledge that Jesus Christ is Lord (sovereign God), to the glory of God the Father. Phillipians 2: 5-11

Useful facts regarding Adam's Fall

Falling: The Background

- *Sin is the violation of God's Word, which is Gods law.*
- *Rebellion against God's Word is sin, which leads to death.*
- *Sin and death require separation from God.*
- *Adam incurred the debt of eternal death when he entered, willingly, into Satan's sinful rebellion against God (although Adam's entry into the rebellion was not intentional).*
- *Adam's death required immediate "spirit" disconnection from God,*
- *God is Spirit, and God the Father's Spirit will not be touched by death, as the Pure Source of Life (Executive of His Community of One, but He sent His Word to rescue Adam).*

Fallen: Satan Takes Possession of God's Property

- *Satan takes possession of Adam—God's original property.*
- *Satan takes **God's** life when he takes Adam into his possession through death.*
- *Since Adam willfully entered into enemy territory, he was guilty. Adam needed a Savior to rescue him out. He had entered into sin through rebellion, and the penalty for sin is death. So a Perfect sacrifice had to be offered to cover Adam's wrong.*

The Defiled Fallen: Adam is unqualified to rescue himself out of eternal death

- *Adam is created pure and undefiled by sin.*

- *God deposits into Adam pure blood that becomes contaminated by sin and death.*
- *Adam, since defiled by sin and death, cannnot present himself as a pure, unblemished sacrifice to satisfy God's requirement for a Pure Life to be offered, as payment for Adam's sin.*

The Qualified Rescuer: Second Adam comes to Adam's rescue

- *The only death that can satisfy God's Divine Justice for a Perfect Sacrifice is a Perfect Sacrifice. Thus, the Second Adam leaves heaven and arrives to the earth as a Substitue/ Substitutionary Death offered by a Pure Life.*
- *Second Adam presents Himself to God on the Cross, on Adam's behalf, to pay his debt to sin which is death.*
- *God's Son, the Second Adam, is God's Word made Flesh.*
- *Neither a piece of fruit, nor a fig leaf (no blood/of the earth) is adequate to deal with a life/death debt problem that requires blood, and is a non-earthly "spiritual" problem. So God replaces Adam and Eve's fig leaves with animal sins to symbolize the coming of His Son who would shed blood as the Perfect Sacrificial Lamb for humanity. For without the shedding of blood there is no forgiveness of sin.*

Temporary Arrangements: Until the coming of "The Lamb," animals are used to cover humanity's sins

- *Based on God's Time-Line of Eternal Events, it would take an extended period of time between Adam's fall and the coming of His Son to the earth.*

- *Lambs, rams, and other animals cover humanity's sin temporarily, first through offerings brought to God from individuals (i.e. Cain and Abel).*
- *The high priests offer pure animals (having never sinned and thus, have non-corrupted blood) up to God on behalf of God's people.*
- *The Lamb of God, God's High Priest, Jesus Christ, eliminates the need for any further animal sacrifice when His Pure Sacrifice is delivered once and for all for the sins of God's people.*

"There is a fountain filled with blood" Lyrics by William Cowper (1731-1800)

"Just As I Am" lyrics by Mahalia Jackson

"Jesus Paid it All" lyrics by Elvina M. Hall

"Mary Had a Little Lamb" lyrics by Sarah Josephina Hale (1830)

Coming Soon to a Bookstore in Your Area—

AMONGUS—Resurrection Power Man!

He came **Among Us!**

from *The Resurrection Power Man Super Children's Series*
©Copyrights pending for the names AMONGUS
and Resurrection Power Man, E.C. Bell, 2019

By E.E. Blessings

After First Man Adam falls into an Eternal problem—to rescue His fallen brother from the clutches of sinful death. Heaven's real-life Super-Hero, Amongus, exchanges His Crown of Glory for a Crown of Thorns. In one single blow to the plan of the Evil 1, Amongus takes the sting out of death, robs the grave of its victory, and then ascends back to His Father to prepare for the sequel—His Second Coming! One day, He will return to rule over the earth. Amongus needs **you** to join His "Resurrection Power Squad!"

While the delivery of this exciting Bible-based plot is similar to a comic-book narrative, it transcends fiction. Super-Hero Amongus is real, and He's preparing to gather His Father's children home. Are you ready? Set? To go join Him in the sky? And then come back to the earth to help him fight, rule and reign?

He made the bird! He Resurrected Faster than a plane! He's "Resurrection Power Man!!!"

About the Author

E. C. Bell is a musician and educator who says the credentials earned for writing *Last Minute Emails to God from a Dying Unbeliever Dear God: Which Way Is Up?* is an eternal perspective that comes from digging deeply into *God's Treasure Chest of Good News*. Inspired by the understanding that the curse of Adam's sin must be broken during one's life to be broken at the time of one's death and is needed, especially at this time. Author unfolds a stirring message of hope. "The idea of any soul perishing stirs me to share the promise of eternal life made by the Second Adam, God's Son. I did not write *Emails* for those who want to argue, but for those who want to receive."

Contact Information: (415) 871-4004.

CPSIA information can be obtained
at www.ICGtesting.com
Printed in the USA
LVHW090244120121
676270LV00008B/27

9 781640 882